Dress, Body, Culture

Series Editor **Joanne B. Eicher,** *Regents' Professor, University of Minnesota*

Advisory Board:

Books in this provocative series seek to articulate the connections between culture and dress which is defined here in its broadest possible sense as any modification or supplement to the body. Interdisciplinary in approach, the series highlights the dialogue between identity and dress, cosmetics, coiffure, and body alterations as manifested in practices as varied as plastic surgery, tattooing, and ritual scarification. The series aims, in particular, to analyze the meaning of dress in relation to popular culture and gender issues and will include works grounded in anthropology, sociology, history, art history, literature, and folklore.

ISSN: 1360-466X

Previously published titles in the Series

305,3
Y68

DRESS, BODY, CULTURE

Women Who Become Men

Albanian Sworn Virgins

Antonia Young

Oxford • New York

First published in 2000 by
Berg
Editorial offices:
150 Cowley Road, Oxford, OX4 1JJ, UK
838 Broadway, Third Floor, New York, NY 10003-4812, USA

Berg is an imprint of Oxford International Publishers Ltd.

Library of Congress Cataloging-in-Publication Data
A catalogue record for this book is available from the Library of Congress.

British Library Cataloguing-in-Publication Data
A catalogue record for this book is available from the British Library.

ISBN   1 85973 335 2 (Cloth)
         1 85973 340 9 (Paper)

Typeset by JS Typesetting, Wellingborough, Northants.
Printed in the United Kingdom by Biddles Ltd, Guildford and King's Lynn.

To my family who have been so encouraging and supportive through-out the years that this has taken to *start*. There will be no end.

And, I hope, to preserve a record for future generations of Albanians, of a culturally respected phenomenon which in the present-day turmoil may soon disappear.

Contents

Acknowledgments

I am indebted to many for advice, assistance and encouragement in completing this study. The idea was first suggested by my husband, Professor Nigel Young, who has encouraged me all through the processes of collecting and recording my research. Professor Emeritus Mildred Dickemann (now Professor Emeritus Jeffrey Martin Dickemann) gave me further encouragement and direction. I am most indebted to Marita and Tonin Naraçi and to Pjeter and Maralba Jani, both for their generous hospitality and continual assistance in making and understanding important contacts and connections. Substantial editing as well as contributions especially in the sphere of gender and Russian translations, were performed by Lucy Young, finer editing and proofreading by Phyllis Young. Ann Christine Eek supplied continual support and advice as well as several magnificent photographs. Chloë Young provided new perspectives especially while filming interviews with 'sworn virgins' themselves, during our visit to Albania in 1996. Additional contacts and inspiration resulted from my participation in the Eighteenth Seminar of Albanian Language, Literature and Culture held in Tirana in August 1996, at the generous invitation of Professors Bahri Beci and Zejnullah Rrahmani and from participation in the SOROS Albanian language course at the invitation of Professors Valentina Duka and Rahmi Memushaj. More recently I have benefitted greatly from the leadership of the Director Stephanie Schwandner-Sievers of Albanian Studies at the University of London and invitations to participate in seminars and conferences held there within the School of Slavonic and East European Studies. Others who have supplied helpful contributions are Dr John Allcock (Head of the Research Unit in South East European Studies, Bradford University), Phyllis Berry, Chris Bowers (with the maps), Dr. Wendy Bracewell, Kimete Bytyçi, Joan Counihan, Van Christo (Frosina Foundation), Dr Robert Elsie, Professor Victor Friedman, Arjan Gjonca (on demographic figures), Isuf Hajrizi (former Editor of *Illyria*), Professor Emeritus Joel Halpern, Dr John Hodgson, Dr John Horton, Martin Hurt, Artan Karini, Professor Dr Karl Kaser, Professor Barbara Kerewesky-Halpern, Sokol Kondi, Edi Kurtezi, Mimoza Lacej, Ludmilla Buxhelli, Marko Milivojević, Heather Minnion, Dorothy Noland, Marcia Oxford, Rafaela Prifti, Professor Agim Prodani, Peter Rennie (Secretary of the Anglo-Albanian Association), Merita Selmanllari, Professor Nancy Ries,

Professor Marjorie Senechal, Rosie Swale, Janie Vinson, Jelka Vince-Pallua, Lala Meredith-Vula (with her account of Raba), Julie Wheelright, John Wood, Philip Wynn, Ferhat Ymeri and Leonora Zefi, and most especially all those proud people, living according to traditional law whom I met and who both offered me generous hospitality and explained what their life-changing decisions have meant to them. I have appreciated the co-operation of my editor Kathryn Earle.

Whilst I have received much help and advice, I know that there will still be errors and omissions which I have overlooked, and shall be glad to be informed of them. The subject matter is ever changing . . .

Note

The place-names included in the text are in the language of the country in which they are located at the time of writing. The exception is Kosov@, a newly evolved term avoiding bias towards the Serbian 'Kosovo' or the Albanian 'Kosova'.

For the sake of uniformity, I have only used masculine pronouns for the 'sworn virgins' when these were used in reported speech referring to any of my subjects. In all other cases I have used feminine pronouns, even where this was avoided by everyone else.

List of Maps and Illustrations

Map 1. Albania's Balkan Frontiers.

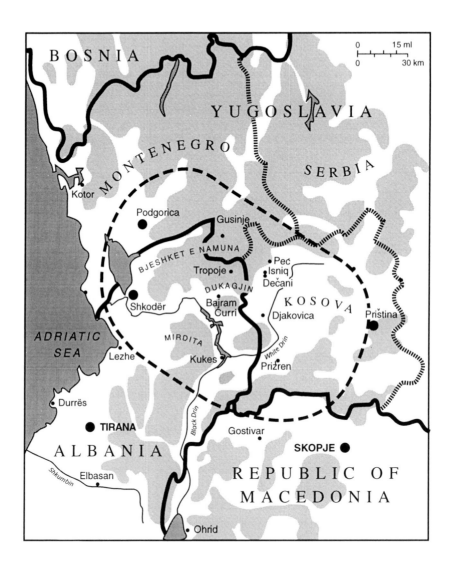

Map 2. The Albanian centre of Europe. The area enclosed by the dotted line marks, very approximately, the area in which most of the 'sworn virgins' mentioned in the text live or have lived.

Preface

'You may . . . find that some of the very things you consider poor and backward
look very different to outside eyes.'

> Marjorie Senechal, *Long Life to Your Children!*
> *A Portrait of High Albania*[1]

It was my brother's trip to Yugoslavia in 1954 which first sparked my interest
to visit and see for myself the rebuilding of a country which had lost 10
percent of its population in the Second World War (more than half were killed
in civil strife at that time). I was inspired, as were many, by the vision of
national and international Youth Brigades building roads and railways, and
the reported enthusiasm and excitement this evoked. E.P. Thompson was one
such volunteer:

> The unusual thing about this railway is the way in which it was built. It is a Youth
> Railway. People in England when they first heard about a Youth Railway thought
> it was some sort of practical game or a propaganda stunt . . . But there were no
> toy trains on the Youth Railway Samac-Sarajevo . . . most of the work went on
> without supervision and with only the most primitive tools . . . The work was
> driven forward, not by threats or by personal incentives, but by songs and an
> amazing spirit of co-operative will . . . (The book documents) what we saw in
> Yugoslavia while we worked among the 'brigaders' (*sic*) on the Railway; what we
> heard when we talked and argued with everyone from distinguished lecturers and
> youth leaders to cooks, clerks and schoolboys; what we felt when we danced the
> *kolo*, shouted or sang with our friends around the bonfires in the evenings.[2]

Post-War[3] Western education in the 1940s and 1950s had given no place to
Eastern Europe. When the realization of its existence opened it up to me, my
fascination grew as I unsystematically read whatever came my way on the
subject. One of the first books I read was Rebecca West's *Black Lamb and
Grey Falcon*,[4] describing her journeys all over Yugoslavia during the years
1937 and 1938. Although West's view is considerably influenced by her Serb
travel companions, she provides a wealth of insight into the Yugoslavia of the
time. Literary critic Larry Woolf stresses the importance of this work as a
prophecy of times ahead:

Almost fifty years after its initial publication *Black Lamb and Grey Falcon* aston-ishes us by the weight and depth of what Rebecca West knew about Yugoslavia, but above all it overwhelms us with the passionate urgency of her need to know, our need to know . . . When *Black Lamb and Grey Falcon* was published in 1941, Hitler made himself the master of Eastern Europe, Yugoslavia had been bombed and abolished, and Rebecca West found that she had been a visitor to a now lost world. At that moment in history, Rebecca West's book challenged Britain and America to cherish an image of Europe in its full moral and political dimensions, to recognize unequivocally that Eastern Europe was a necessary part of Europe . . . Our challenge will be to discover Eastern Europe anew, and recognize it without the ideological marks that have served for simple identification, our challenge will be to accept it as part of Europe, and not the lesser part.[5]

In the 1950s and 1960s I took the opportunity to visit Yugoslavia whenever I could, travelling by all means: boat,[6] bus, foot, hitch-hiking, sometimes on ox-carts, and by train. One of the trains was the *mali ćiro*[7] which took seventeen hours to chug the fifty-eight kilometres from Gostivar to Ohrid. The tiny three-coached train moved so slowly up the mountains that it was possible to get out and pick blackberries alongside and get back on the moving train. In earlier times when there were three classes, only the first-class passengers were permitted to remain in the moving train as it climbed the mountains. Second-class passengers had to get out and walk, while the third-class passengers had to get out and push the train. I was shown the handlebars on the outside of the coaches for this purpose. When the train came off its tracks a couple of times along the journey everyone got out to heave it back on again.

With a Yugoslav friend I spent a summer camping in all six republics,[8] experiencing the fascinating differences which even Tito's enforced cohesion could not homogenize. Generally I was not believed when I claimed to be British on the Macedonian bank of Lake Ohrid as I looked across to Albania on the other side in 1958. At that time very few tourists left the magnificent Dalmatian coast to travel inland; those who did were French or German families or groups. My appearance, the fact that I was travelling alone and my use of sufficient Serbo-Croatian to be sometimes thought of as belonging to a different one of the Yugoslav republics combined to make more plausible a life story involving an Albanian childhood and escape[9] to Yugoslavia by swimming across the lake. I later gazed at Albania from Corfu after a journey down the coast by boat. Yugoslavia had long since broken its links with Albania: when Tito fell out with the demands of the Soviet Union in 1948, previous considerations of Albania becoming a seventh republic of Yugoslavia ended.

Marriage, emigration and family ties kept me from visiting Yugoslavia during the height of its prosperity and hope in the 1970s, but when I returned (shortly after Tito's death in 1980) it was with new purpose. My husband's work in Peace Studies took us to the Inter-University Centre in Dubrovnik to share the running of international conferences and courses on nonviolence and peace education. The Centre, housed in a fine building dating from the days of Austro-Hungarian domination, was an institute which could welcome students and faculty from both East and West, offering a place for interaction between people of Communist and non-Communist backgrounds. Cynics might question the validity of the work which was not able to help prevent the appalling killing and destruction of the 1990s, but it is worth mentioning that the staff of the Centre continued work throughout the worst times, despite a direct hit on the building and devastating fire. With international support, the Centre re-opened after only a short break with renewed course offerings.

The republication in the mid-1980s of the liveliest of Mary Edith Durham's seven books on the Balkans, *High Albania*[10] brought recognition back to her work.[11] This remarkable British woman (usually known as Edith Durham) travelled in the Balkans during the first quarter of the twentieth century becoming ever more involved as an artist, self-trained anthropologist and relief work organizer, as well as informed political commentator, even influencing British foreign policy in the area.[12]

Born in 1863, she did not visit the Balkans until the age of thirty-seven. By that time she was tiring in her task of nursing her ailing mother, and was advised by her doctor to have a break to 'get right away no matter where, as long as the change is complete'. She took a Lloyds steamer from Trieste, followed the recommendation of someone on board and disembarked at Kotor in Montenegro. Thereafter in the following years she travelled extensively all over the Balkans campaigning vigorously for the independence of the many minority populations.

In times of war and tribal revolts she took medical aid, food and blankets to the victims: she always tried to hear all sides of the many conflicts with which she came into contact, and to publicize these situations. A comment she made in 1913 could, unfortunately, well be repeated today: 'The one thing that can be said with certainty is that no permanent solution of the Balkan Question has been arrived at.'[13] After her first visits to Montenegro and Serbia, Durham took up the cause of the Albanians[14] and subsequently all her writing related to their various situations, political, historical and anthropological.

In a speech during a celebration for her eightieth birthday, Durham commented: 'It occurred to me that the vexed questions of Balkan politics might be solved by studying the manners and customs of each district, and so learning to whom each place should really belong. I cheerfully started on this vast programme.' The result of this endeavour is her *Some Tribal Origins, Laws and Customs of the Balkans*, which is unrivalled for its graphically written anthropological detail on human groups and phenomena, many of which no longer exist.[15] One such phenomenon – and the focus of this book – which Durham observed was that of the 'sworn virgin'; she met at least nine of them.

If nurturing three children limited my Balkan travels, it also opened up several new dimensions. One of these was the writings of Laura Ingalls Wilder whose series of nine children's books I shared with my own daughters. Later the stories were poorly adapted and serialized on television under the title 'Little House on the Prairie'.[16] These relate the true life story of Laura, her parents and three sisters as they moved across America during the latter half of the nineteenth century, forever searching a self-sufficient life. In the last of these books Laura (married in the previous book) and her husband, faced new disasters and were unable to care for their baby, Rose. Such an unsatisfactory end to two years' reading left me anxious to discover what became of these real people.

I was able to follow the story quite unexpectedly. Based in Norway in 1983, I had the good fortune through the Peace Research Institute of Oslo, to become acquainted with the Norwegian anthropologist, Berit Backer[17] who had just completed her Ph.D thesis on Albanian kinship systems. At the time of pursuing her fieldwork, in the mid-1970s, foreigners were not permitted to conduct any independent study in Albania. Instead, Backer managed to obtain permission to work in the all-Albanian village of Isniq, in Kosov@,[18] two miles outside Dečani, close to the Albanian border. Her bibliography included *The Peaks of Shala: Being a Record of Certain Wanderings Among the Hill-Tribes of Albania* by Rose Wilder Lane.[19] This I discovered was indeed Laura's baby Rose who became an avid reader as a child, and took the unusual step for a teenage girl at that time of leaving the rural mid-West to become a journalist. In 1915 she was based in San Francisco, where she was briefly married. By the 1920s it was claimed that she was the best- paid woman writer in the world.[20]

In 1919 Rose was commissioned by the Red Cross to report on the situation of refugees in Europe after the First World War. Through this work she was invited by friends setting up schools in the mountains of northern Albania, to join one of their expeditions. This became the inspiration for her book, published just a decade after Durham's *High Albania*. More romantic and less detailed in ethnographic documentation than Durham's, Lane's *Peaks of Shala* nevertheless confirms many of the traditions which Durham had already noted. One of these is the phenomenon of the 'sworn virgin' (Durham's 'Albanian virgin').

There is extensive literature on travel in Albania, much written by early foreign visitors to the area in the nineteenth and twentieth centuries and up to the Second World War. It includes works by such prominent figures as Lord Byron and Edward Lear.[21] Almost all these writers referred to the *Kanun* (the Code of laws collected by Lekë Dukagjini in the fifteenth century), and many to 'Albanian virgins'. Lane does not write of actually having met one, but records having been assumed to be one! The tribal chief Lulash of Thethi interpreted the combination of her travelling without a husband, dressed in trousers and sporting short hair as indications that she had taken the vow.[22] More widely documented in the past,[23] the phenomenon known as the 'sworn virgin' was thought to have been eradicated under the Communist regime. This became an aspect of Albanian culture that I wanted to pursue.

A conference held at Bradford University in 1987 on 'Women Travellers in the Balkans' prompted me to present a paper on Rose Wilder Lane,[24] and to speculate whether 'sworn virgins' still existed. When I first visited northern Albania in 1989, I made enquiries concerning this question. Western visitors to Albania at that time were only permitted to travel inside the country in diligently supervised, strictly guarded, but very well cared for groups along specific, well-prepared routes. These groups were forbidden to speak to anyone other than their tour guides or government representatives. The foreigners were informed of the wonders of the Communist era: illiteracy had been reduced from 85 per cent (even higher amongst women) before the War of Liberation (as the Second World War was referred to in Albania) to 5 per cent, no-one earned more than twice as much as anyone else, there were no taxes, no crime, no unemployment and rents were less than 10 per cent of income; furthermore, five-year plans from the 1970s had completed the electrification of the villages.

Only in later years did we hear the full cost of Albania's 'progress'. In the interests of this progress, besides the horrors which are widely known about today, many books were burnt, many banned. There were no town plans or road maps available, such was the concern of the strict Stalinist regime to keep the ordinary people in ignorance concerning anything outside their immediate domain. Little wonder then, that while few in the North, and fewer still in the South, knew that the tradition of 'sworn virgin' was still alive, recognition even of the concept was almost unheard of only a hundred miles away in Albania's capital, Tirana. This partly reflects an unwillingness of urban and aspiring Albanians to acknowledge the survival of traditions, on the other hand it goes without saying that this part of Europe is undergoing a profound and rapid change which seems likely to transform both the context and the very existence of the phenomenon described in this study.

Figure 1. 'Here we found one of the Albanian virgins who wear male attire. While we halted to water the horses she came up – a lean, wiry, active woman of forty-seven, clad in very ragged garments, breeches and coat.' (Durham (1909), *High Albania*, p. 80). Edith Durham: Rapsha, c. 1908

Notes

1. Senechal, M. (1997), *Long Life to Your Children! A Portrait of High Albania*, Amherst, Massachusetts: University of Massachusetts Press, p.37.

2. Thompson, E.P. (ed.) (1948), *The Railway: An Adventure in Construction*, London: The British-Yugoslav Association, pp. viii–x.

3. For anyone born in the three decades following 1930, 'The War' referred to the Second World War, for those born earlier it was 'The Last War'.

4. West, R. (1982), *Black Lamb and Grey Falcon: A Journey Through Yugoslavia*, London: Macmillan. (First published in 1941).

5. Woolf, L. (Feb. 1991), 'Let's Listen this Time', *New York Review of Books*.

6. This was before the road had been built down the Dalmatian coast.

7. Built during the First World War by German troops, this narrow gauge railway still used its original rolling stock until it ceased operation in 1966.

8. Slovenia, Croatia, Serbia, Bosnia-Herzigovina, Montenegro and Macedonia.

9. During the years 1945–90 few Albanians were given permission to make visits outside their country.

10. Durham, M.E. (1909), *High Albania*, London: Edward Arnold. Republished and edited by John Hodgson in 1985 in London: Virago Press; and in 1987 in Boston: Beacon Press. Hodgson's new introduction provided the fullest biography of Durham to that date. See also Hodgkinson, H. (1995), 'Edith Durham and the Formation of the Albanian State' in Young, A. (ed.), *Albania and the Surrounding World: Papers from the British-Albanian Colloquium, South East European Studies Association held at Pembroke College, Cambridge, 29th–31st March, 1994*, Bradford: Research Unit in South East European Studies, University of Bradford, pp. 14–23.

11. Since this time, reference to her works appear in a large proportion of books published on the Balkans, and she has been the subject of several dissertations, for example: Jolley, L. (1988), *Mary Edith Durham: Her Life, Her Travelling and Her Collecting in the Balkans*, BA (Hon.), Manchester: Manchester Polytechnic; MacKenzie, P. (1993), *Mary Edith Durham (l863-1944): Traveller and Collector in the Balkans*; van Hal, T. (1991), *Reizen en schrijven: een onderzoek naar het werk van Mary Edith Durham* (Travel and text: the writings of Mary Edith Durham), MA, Amsterdam: University of Amsterdam, which includes a complete bibliography of all Durham's writing. There are five museums in Britain which contain her collections: the Bankfield Museum in Halifax which received the bulk of her costume and textile collection with some related images, and which devotes a whole room to these collections and to other relevant photographs, maps and artifacts portraying Durham's life and work in her areas of concern; the Cambridge Museum of Archaeology and Anthropology (jewelry and amulets); the Museum of Mankind in London (largely manuscripts, plus a small collection of objects); the Pitt-Rivers Museum in Oxford (jewelry, silver-handled weapons, musical instruments); and the Royal Anthropological Institute (photographs). The Bankfield Museum has produced two catalogues relating to their holdings of Durham exhibits: Start, L.E. (1977), with notes by M. Edith Durham, Halifax: Calderdale Museums; and (1997), *Bread, Salt*

and Our Hearts, Halifax: Calderdale Council. Several of Durham's letters, written to Foreign Office officials of the time are kept at the Public Records Office in Kew (London).

12. See Hodgkinson (1995), 'Edith Durham and the Formation of the Albanian State', pp. 22–4.

13. Durham, M.E. (1914), *The Struggle for Scutari*, London: Edward Arnold.

14. Vesna Goldsworthy points out that Durham was unusual among British writers, openly to change her Balkan allegiance; see Goldsworthy, V. (1998), *Inventing Ruritania: The Imperialism of the Imagination*, New Haven; London: Yale University Press, p. 165.

15. Durham, M.E. (1928), *Some Tribal Origins, Laws and Customs of the Balkans*, London: Allen & Unwin. This is still considered the most thorough documentation of tribal life in the Albanian lands written in English.

16. The books give proof of the extreme difficulty facing even the most hard-working in trying to make ends meet. The Homesteading Act of 1861, extremes of weather and such disasters as locust plagues and prairie fires combined to make life very tough for the American pioneers. See also Holtz, W.V. (1993), *The Ghost in the Little House: a Life of Rose Wilder Lane*, Columbia, Missouri; London: University of Missouri Press, 1993, pp. 3–8.

17. Sadly Berit was murdered in her home town, Oslo, Norway in 1993. Her funeral was attended by, amongst others, 1,000 Kosovar Albanians who hired coaches to be there.

18. This recently adopted spelling has become the accepted neutral form indicating the region known in Albanian as Kosova, and Serbian as Kosovo.

19. Lane, R.W. (1922,3), *The Peaks of Shala: Being a Record of Certain Wanderings among the Hill-Tribes of Albania*, London: Chapman & Dodd; New York: Harper Bros. Translated into Albanian: Lein, R.U. (1997), *Majat e Shalës*, Prishtina: Rilindja.

20. Personal correspondence with William Holtz.

21. See Duka, V. (1995), 'Albania as viewed by English Travellers of the Nineteenth Century', in Young, A. (ed.), *Albania and the Surrounding World: Papers from the British Albanian Colloquium, South East European Studies Association held at Pembroke College, Cambridge 29th–31st March, 1994*, Bradford: Research Unit in South East European Studies, University of Bradford, pp. 1–21; Mema, S. (1987), *Albanica I*, Tirana: Biblioteka Kombetare, Secktori i Albanologjise; Goldsworthy, V. (1998), *Inventing Ruritania*. For an extensive bibliography of women writers on the Balkans, see Jennifer Finder's chapter 14, 'Women Travellers in the Balkans: A Bibliographical Guide' in Allcock, J.B. and Young A. (eds) (1991), *Black Lambs and Grey Falcons: Women Travellers in the Balkans*, Bradford: Bradford University Press, pp. 192–201. Republication (forthcoming 2000), Oxford; New York: Berghahn).

22. Lane (1923), *Peaks of Shala*, pp. 207–8.

23. The well-known Albanian ethnologist, Andromaqi Gjergji collected documentation of 'sworn virgins' published up to the date when she herself met one in 1952. See: Gjergj, A. (1963), 'Gjurmë të Matriarkatit më disa Doke të Dikurshme të

Jetës Familjare' (Traces of Matriarchy in Some Former Customs of Family Life), *Buletini i Universitetit Shtetëror të Tiranës (Shkencat Shoqërore)*, no. 2, pp. 284–92. Several German and Austrian ethnographers and diplomats also reported on the phenomenon.

24. Young, A. (1991), 'Rose Wilder Lane, 1886–1968', Chapter nine in J.B. Allcock and A. Young (eds), *Black Lambs and Grey Falcons*, pp. 90–101.

Figure 2. Shkurtan scything. AY: village outside Bajram Curri, 1994

_1_

Introduction

The conditions and basic necessities on which the society was formed have maintained the social phenomenon of the 'sworn virgin': 'It exists not as a fossil, but as an expression of the varied economic methods in this patriarchal society.'

M. Bajraktarović, 'The Problem of *Tobelije*'.[1]

The Albanians

The population of Albania is one of the most homogenous in all the Balkans: 91 per cent are ethnic Albanians, 7 per cent Greeks, 2 per cent Vlachs, Bulgarians, Macedonians, Montenegrins, Roma and Serbs. Albania's population has multiplied almost three times since 1939 when there were just over one million inhabitants to its present of approximately 3.3 million.[2] It is claimed to be the only country where as many of its population lives just outside its own borders (in Montenegro, Kosov@ (between 1974 and 1990 an autonomous province of Yugoslavia), Macedonia and Greece) as within them.

A brief Historical Background

Much that is claimed concerning the origins of the peoples now inhabiting the Balkans has not been unequivocally determined. The name 'Albania'[3] is believed to be derived from the Albanoi, an Illyrian tribe that lived in what is today central Albania at least from the second century BC. The present-day Albanian lands have been a crossroads for world interaction and trade. During the seventh to fifth centuries BC, Greek colonists, mainly from Corfu and Corinth, settled alongside the indigenous Illyrian populations. The Roman conquest in the second century BC transformed the economy into an agricultural one. The Via Egnatia, built in the second century BC provided a trade route between Europe and Asia: it linked the cities of Apollonia and Dyrrachium (Durrës) on the coast, through Elbasan to Constantinople and

_1_

the Middle East. Edwin Jacques[4] comments on the difficulty of finding clear historical documentation:

> The absence of early Albanian documents has left us only dim traces of their beginnings. It is possible that over 200 generations of unnamed Albanians have lived and labored, loved and hated, married and begotten, struggling continually for survival. They suffered frequent desperate want. They sought to improve their condition, they perpetuated their language and their culture, and they usually died with little to show for the struggle. These magnificent Albanians have continued their dramatic struggle for seventy centuries but have recorded for posterity only the last three of these. The many preceding silent centuries allow us only occasional and fleeting glimpses of the heroic past of these largely unknown people.[5]

By the second century AD, the native population had become known as Arbërs, and when the Roman Empire split in AD 395, Arbëria became part of the Eastern or Byzantine Empire. It has been argued that by the eleventh century a distinctly Albanian society had crystallized. By the fourteenth century this society, weakened by internal crisis and external attack, was transformed into a feudal one, and by the end of that century several noble families dominated Albania, amongst them the Dukagjini in the north. The country was later threatened with a new and more serious invasion from the Ottoman Empire. Albania's national hero, Skanderbeg,[6] whose leadership for forty years gave Albania its only independence in half a millennium, was killed in 1468.

Under Ottoman occupation for the next 450 years, there followed periodic mass conversions to Islam, and also frequent Albanian uprisings and extensive emigration to surrounding countries. Since the sixteenth century, the Albanians have called their language *shqip*, their country *Shqipëria* and themselves *shqiptarë*.[7]

Albania's isolation both physically and politically has been an important factor in shaping its history, which in turn is important for our topic: the 'sworn virgins'.

Until the 1920s, up to 30 per cent of the male population died violent deaths as a result of bloodfeuds (see Appendix 2 for detailed discussion), putting an especially high value on male descendants. Not infrequently the shortage of boys was redressed by designating a daughter henceforth to become a son (a 'sworn virgin').

From the 1920s, the self-declared King Zog I ruled with increasing dependence on Italy until Italy's invasion in 1939 at which time Zog fled the country, never to return.

The War and After

During the Second World War, in 1941, Enver Hoxha[8] emerged as the first leader of the Albanian Communist Party. His power increased throughout the five decades of his leadership. He implemented more and more extreme measures to carry out his form of Stalinism, surrounding himself with supporters and dealing harshly with any opposition or feared competition, even ordering the death of many former friends.[9] During this time, between 1945 and 1991, Albanians were not permitted to travel outside the country unless on official government business. Any attempt to leave was considered treasonable, resulting in imprisonment, exile or even death, threatening not only the individual, but the whole extended family. Nor were people allowed even to leave their area of residence without permission. These factors combined to keep the population very static while its size rose dramatically.

Rural dwellers became more and more impoverished as the parcels of land they were permitted to own and work for themselves declined to minimal or non-existent amounts. There was an attempt to provide rudimentary health care all over the country, although the service in no way lived up to the quality or quantity that the propaganda of the day publicized. Albania was declared an atheist state in 1967, backed up by intense religious persecution.[10]

Prohibition was applied to the practicing of religion: to strengthen the atheist argument, Hoxha revived the words of the publicist and writer Pashko Vasa, 'the religion of Albania is Albanianism.'[11]

Life After Communism

After major demonstrations, but remarkably little violence, on 11 December 1990, opposition parties were legalized. There was however violence against symbols of the state: government buildings and all means of public transport countrywide were set alight, windows were smashed, papers and records burned; this extended also to schools, children following the example of their elders. It was also the fate of factories, co-operative farming enterprises including vineyards, olive and citrus groves which were burned, greenhouses and irrigation systems were vandalized.[12] Many Albanians, mostly from central and southern Albania, emigrated to Greece and Italy to work for exploitative wages. There was little investment in the land, much of which was left untended.

Religion was finally legalized again late in 1990. Current estimates claim that, as before the War, Albania's population is made up of approximately 70 per cent Muslim, 10 per cent Catholic living in the North, the remaining

20 per cent Orthodox living primarily in the South.[13] Northern Albania has much in common with Kosov@. Geg is spoken in both these areas, whereas Tosk is the Albanian dialect of the South.

When the Democratic Party was voted in to power in 1992 with Sali Berisha as President, the concept of a civil society barely surfaced in the race to become Westernized. By opening the door to democracy it also opened the floodgates to corruption. Berisha's increasingly totalitarian behaviour and alleged involvement in, or at least acceptance of, the growing corruption led to deepening divisions in society. The economy was ravaged by the fraudulent 'pyramid' investment schemes which were seen to be supported by the government – members of which were suspected to be beneficiaries of the schemes. The collapse of these schemes and Berisha's refusal to resign as President, led to widespread violence and anarchy in the first months of 1997. The opening up of armouries all over the country provided the population with an estimated one million lethal weapons. International concern led to the demand for a general election as a pre-condition to the provision of foreign aid. The Socialists, elected into government in the summer of 1997, hoped to control the violence.

The Focus of the Study

The purpose of this book is to place the unique phenomenon of Albanian 'sworn virgins': honorary men, surviving mostly in remote areas of northern Albania, within the context of Albanian culture and society generally. In the following study I will attempt to summarize the various accounts of these women (since 1989) and to compare different anthropological and ethnographic explanations and analyses of them and their status. The elucidation of some aspects of Albania's unique history will help to contextualize how the phenomenon has evolved and remains an integral part of this society. By adding new findings from my own field studies and in-depth interviews with a number of these people in northern Albania in the past decade, I consider the way in which dress demarcates gender status in a strongly patriarchal society. That dress plays an important part in the cultural construction of gender is evident at significant events such as weddings and property transfers, or marking property boundaries. The choice of dress reflects the nature of a particular socio-economic system in highland Albania and some other parts of the Balkans and represents a particular and often harsh environment in which clothing and honour are connected to economic exigencies. It is the economic factor which is crucial to the need for certain women in this patriarchal society to take a man's role in order to head an otherwise maleless

Figure 3. Pashke with relative, in courtyard outside house of wedding reception. Note contrast of Pashke's male clothing and stance (despite her diminutive size), with that of her female relative wearing a long skirt, apron and white socks. AY: Okolo, 1993

family. Furthermore these women, as men, are prepared to take up arms[14] if necessary in order to contribute to the control by which family honour is maintained: the bloodfeud.[15]

With the current interest in the West in gender theory and in particular dress and cross-dressing, the ways in which these women-who-become-men have taken men's roles, and their symbols of masculinity, as compared with traditional womens' dress in its wider sense (as set out in Chapter 9), will be part of the focus. For most 'sworn virgins' male clothing is clearly emancipatory. The dress of the Albanian women and, contrastingly, that of the 'sworn virgins', especially in a rural setting, demarcates not only sex but status – and explains gender status in particular. With a change in dress there are enormous pressures to conform to conventional gender roles as defined by that culture. Yet gender identity is not necessarily linked to sexual preference. The role of dress in Albania is changing rapidly and new forms of individual and collective identity are emerging.

There is a real danger of projecting the sexual perspectives of leisured Western societies on a culture such as this. The phenomenon of 'sworn virgins' sparks little interest within Albania itself. Most Albanians are eager to see 'progress' towards Western lifestyles which they seek to emulate. When I first began my research, few outside northern Albania had ever heard of the 'sworn virgin' tradition; those who had heard of it believed it no longer existed, many vehemently denied the possibility. I found in Tirana, amongst those who considered themselves to have broken with tradition, some Albanian men felt threatened by the idea, and some women were positively disgusted, calling it 'unnatural'; a response which they applied even more adamantly to female homosexuality.

This study sets out to be comparative, looking for variations by region, age, historical period, religion and socio-economic status. Are there variations in the relationships of the 'sworn virgins' to the traditional laws (the *Kanun*, and its enactment through the *besa* (oath)) found in specific areas of Albania or more widely in other parts of the Balkans? Is there a solution other than that offered by the 'sworn virgins' to finding a household head when there is no man available to take over the role? Or are there alternative inheritance practises that by-pass this need? How has the phenomenon of the 'sworn virgin' evolved over time? How do the varying lives of those 'sworn virgins' interviewed inform us about such issues as sexuality and procreation, families and kinship in comparative peasant societies, and about these issues within their own culture? Does an Albanian 'sworn virgin' moving into an urban setting renegotiate that traditional and honoured identity? My personal case studies (see especially Lule pp. 70–74 and Dilore pp. 74–76) raise these issues in a highly pertinent way. Does the dress and behaviour of our subjects suggest any links to lesbianism, transsexuality or to transvestism in other cultures? How can we be certain of the absolute abstinence from sexual activity to which they vow? Finally what happened to 'sworn virgins' under Communism, and how does the situation compare to that of the present day? Can the phenomenon survive now that it can be openly studied? Undoubtedly it is changing as the society enters a modern and more homogenous Europe. Will it continue to exist into the new millennium, given the enormous pressures of Westernization, the changing roles of women in Albanian society and the hundreds of thousands of transient Kosovar refugees who were forced into northern Albania?

Cultural Misunderstanding

Since the topics of gender change and sexuality are of considerable interest to the general reader, they are often sensationalized. An example of this was an article which I wrote for *Cosmopolitan*.[16] The article was unfortunately considerably altered when edited, a fact of which I only became aware after its publication. I did follow it up with a document 'Misquotes and Misrepresentations by *Cosmopolitan* in their December Issue on Albania's Sworn Virgins', but the editors were not prepared to publish any part of it. The editorial changes added specific words which are inappropriate when discussing the phenomenon. In particular I had already clarified to the editors that I wanted to avoid words like 'bizarre' and 'sacrifice'. Both these terms were inserted by them making it an ethnocentric report with cultural assumptions about gender roles in that community.[17] *Cosmopolitan*'s editors may have chosen to sensationalize the issue of sacrifice because sex sells in the 1990s, and the notion that these women had to give up their sexuality was interpreted by them as a great personal sacrifice.

In fact the taking of a male role by women in these specifically defined situations in their own country is not only acceptable and highly commendable, but is a choice of a better life – often actively made by these women themselves. Although in some cases swearing the oath was seen as a sacrifice, the connotation of the word is very different in a society where offering one's services for the good of society is considered a positive action, hence if there was sacrifice involved for the woman in becoming a man, this in itself would enhance her self-esteem. This point is brought out particularly by the Russian ethnologist M. Bajraktarović, who himself came from a Communist background, where individual sacrifice for the common good would not be considered a sacrifice as we know it: 'In traditional tribal society, to sacrifice oneself is not only considered a necessity, but honorable and humane.' He therefore emphasizes that 'sworn virgins' in taking the vow of celibacy make a positive sacrifice of their own happiness for that of their families and clans.[18]

As a further example from the *Cosmopolitan* article, my phrase 'they crop their hair short' was changed to 'they shave their heads',[19] giving the reader a very different picture to that which I observed. My stress on the importance of honour was also misconstrued. Other inserted words added to the inauthenticity of my article, for example labeling the Laws of Lek Dukagjini (the *Kanun*) as 'haphazard' and 'anarchic'.[20] Such misunderstanding shows ignor-

Figure 4. Travellers' guide: 'Just ask the fellow his name,' I said to Sabri. 'Fellow?'
he echoed. 'Why, he's a girl!' Bernard Newman: c. 1935

ance of a body of systematic customary law which has gained enormous international respect as a basis from which to study the minutely defined controls of a society as it has lived and been ordered for centuries.[21]

That perceptions change over time can be clearly seen when we read accounts from past decades. As an example it may not have offended readers in 1936 as it would today to learn of Bernard Newman's mode of enquiry into the exact sex of his 'virgin' guide:

> The youth who had guided and guarded us in our descent the previous evening had come to see us off. I thought I ought to have his name for my book.
> 'Just ask the fellow his name,' I said to Sabri.
> 'Fellow?' he echoed. 'Why, he's a girl!'
> 'Rubbish!' I said.
> 'He is a girl!' He turned to the youth: 'Aren't you a girl?' he demanded.
> The youth said: 'Yes.'
> Sabri, noticing my continued disbelief, tore open the 'youth's' shirt and revealed definitely feminine breasts.[22]

Finding the 'Sworn Virgins'

Having read about the existence of 'sworn virgins' earlier in the twentieth century, and hearing that there was at least one still living in northern Albania, I was eager to find out whether the phenomenon had persisted. During the 1990s I returned frequently to Albania and made many good friends there. In particular I spent time in the Naraçi family in Shkodër and they not only provided traditional hospitality, but made great efforts to help me resolve my quest. Thanks to Marita Naraçi, a teacher from Shkodër, my network of informants throughout the villages of northern Albania soon provided leads for me to follow up. The Naraçi family (like many others) was exiled to work in villages far from their home town as a punishment during much of the Communist era, for the crime of their upper-class birth and Catholic upbringing.

It was through Marita Naraçi's enquiries and contacts, that I first confirmed that the tradition was still alive in Albania. Her neighbour, Meri married into a family of whom one was such a person. Meri had been surprised at first, but quickly gained respect for the acceptance which everyone in the relative's village had accorded her.

In 1993 I first had the opportunity to meet a 'sworn virgin'. I travelled alone from Shkodër (Albania's second largest town), took rides aboard a series of trucks, sharing the bare boards with sometimes sixty other standing passengers. Although the distance from Shkodër is only about 50 miles, my

Figure 5. Pashke attending a wedding in smart male attire. AY: Okolo, 1993. A
similar picture of Pashke appears in the *National Geographic*, February
1999

journey took most of the day. I walked the last several miles of rough stony
track along the valley floor, west out of Theth on a hot sunny day in July.
Curious children gathered around me, some leading goats whose bells clinked
alongside us, echoed by others from the mountainsides. We crossed a small
waddi (dried up river-bed) on a rough wooden slatted bridge, avoiding holes
where the slats had rotted, and came immediately into a tiny village. On
asking to meet Pashke, I was led through a small room full of people, where
Pashke was enjoying the social role of a man at a wedding reception (above).
She was seated, holding a glass of wine, a cigarette tucked behind one ear,
dressed in a man's smart shirt and trousers. She smiled broadly, greeted me
warmly and found me a seat next to her, ensuring that I was provided with a
plateful of food.

Following tradition, the bride stood glumly in her bridal finery, eyes
downcast – the epitome of subservience – in this one room of the house
filled with wedding guests eating and drinking from plentiful supplies (the
lavishness of the wedding was expressed by the plates of guests' half-eaten
meat and other food). While wine and beer were provided in great quantity,
drinking water was limited by the size of the single plastic jug and mug passed
to whomever was in need. The room itself, though small, was newly built,
with unplastered walls and a concrete floor. Before the serious drinking began

the bride, the women and children left the room; Pashke remained. As an honoured guest (in Albania *all* guests from afar are honoured) it was insisted that I too should remain with the men to drink some more to the prosperity of the marriage – and to its production of many strong sons!

I was later to find that there are currently a number of women living as men in northern Albania, and I had the opportunity to spend time with several of them; I may unknowingly have met others. The 'sworn virgins' are not always recognizable. Once their parents, or they themselves – usually as children or adolescents – make the vow to become men, they dress and behave accordingly. After years of acting as men, they do take on extraordinarily masculine appearances, not only in their manner of dress, but in their whole body discipline.

Early records refer predominantly to this cross-gender change as the only acceptable alternative to marrying the man to whom a woman had been betrothed, thereby saving the honour of all involved. However, most of my contacts gave as a primary motivation the need for an inheritor and household head where no suitable male was otherwise available. By definition this included the readiness to take action in case of a bloodfeud.[23]

Notes

1. Barjaktarović, M. (1965–6), 'The Problem of *Tobelije*', *Glasnik Ethnografskog Museja*, Belgrade: Knjiga 28–29, p. 132.

2. Until the recent slaughter and forced emigrations, Albanians made up the largest ethnic group after the Serbs within present-day Yugoslavia (Serbia and Montenegro), and also the second largest in Macedonia.

Very approximate distribution of Albanians in Albania and in countries/regions immediately surrounding Albania

Population	Albanian population	% Albanian population
Albania 3,300,000	3,168,000	96
Greece 10,500,000	100,000*	<1
Kosov@ 2,000,000	1,840,000	92
Montenegro 512,000	41,000	8
Macedonia 1,913,000	440,000	23

* This figure is from the Greek 1997 census; it is not compatible with Albanian figures of emigration to Greece, which reached 350,000 by 1999. At the time of writing the 'ethnic cleansing' of Kosovar Albanians has changed the situation in all areas.

3. For a fuller account see Malcolm, N. (1998), *Kosovo: a Short History*, London: Macmillan, p. 29.

4. Jacques (1908–96) was a missionary who taught in Korça between 1932 and 1940.

5. Jacques, E.E. (1995), *The Albanians: an Ethnic History from Prehistoric Times to the Present*, Jefferson, North Carolina; London: McFarland & Company Inc., p. xii. But see also Carver (1998), *The Accursed Mountains: Journeys in Albania*, London: John Murray for a less sympathetic view.

6. Skanderbeg has become Albania's greatest mythologized hero.

7. Some scholars believe that these names are derived from the word *shqiptoj* (to speak intelligibly), others that it originated from the word *shqiponje* (eagle). The double-headed eagle features as a national symbol on the Albanian flag.

8. Enver Hoxha became Europe's most authoritarian Communist leader, as well as the longest in power (from 1945 until his death in 1985).

9. See, for example 'Tefta's Story' in Post, S.E.P. (1998), *Women in Modern Albania*, Jefferson, North Carolina; London: McFarland, pp. 168–9.

10. Unknown numbers of religious leaders were imprisoned, tortured and killed; 2,169 religious institutions were closed, destroyed or turned to other uses, some as museums.

11. Pashko Vasa (1825–92), described himself as 'an Albanian Christian functionary': Vasa, P. (1879), *The Truth on Albania and the Albanians: Historical and Critical*, London: National Press Agency.

12. For a contemporary report, see Young, A. and Prodani, A. (7 Nov. 1992), 'The Bitter Earth', *Illyria*, vol. 2, no. 143.

13. Young, A. (1999), 'Religion and Society in Present-Day Albania', *Journal of Contemporary Religion*, vol. l4, no. 1, pp. 5–16.

14. Backer, B. (1979), *Behind the Stone Walls: changing Household Organization among the Albanians of Kosovo*, Oslo: PRIO-publication S-8/79, p. 208.

15. Whitaker, I. (1968), 'Tribal Structure and National Politics in Albania, 1910–1950', in Lewis, I.M. *History and Social Anthropology*, London; New York: Tavistock Publications, p. 265.

16. Young, A. (Dec. 1995), 'The Sworn Virgins of Albania', *Cosmopolitan*, pp. 44–8.

17. Young, A. (Dec. 1995), 'The Sworn Virgins of Albania', pp. 44–8.

18. Bajraktarović, M. (1965–6), p. 132.

19. Young (Dec. 1995), 'The Sworn Virgins of Albania', p. 44.

20. Young (Dec. 1995), 'The Sworn Virgins of Albania', p. 48.

21. Contributions were made in a panel discussion at the University of London in February 1999 by lawyers, anthropologists and political researchers, on the value of these laws today. The collected papers are to be published as *Albanian Studies Occasional Papers*, no. 1, by the School of Slavonic and East European Studies.

22. Newman, B. (1936), *Albanian Backdoor*, London: Jenkins, pp. 260–1.

23. See Appendix 2 on *The Bloodfeud*.

2

Tree of Blood, Tree of Milk:[1] *Patriarchy and Patricentricity in Rural Albania*

In all its apparent backwardness and poverty, the Balkan world offered British women a chance of real equality with men. British women enjoyed a sort of 'honorary male status' in the Balkans. Many of them took little interest in Balkan women, except in a thoroughly patronising way. Durham, who rarely saw them as anything other than men's chattels and overworked wretches, devoted more attention to the exotic Albanian 'Virgins', the women who dressed as men and vowed never to marry, than to any of the hard-working wives and mothers she met.

V. Goldsworthy, *Inventing Ruritania: the Imperialism of the Imagination*[2]

Goldsworthy's comment exemplifies Durham's (see below) specific concentration on 'sworn virgins' showing her interest in representing a phenomenon that is an exception to the norm in kinship codes.

Tribe, Clan and Kinship

In anthropological terms, rural society in northern Albania is strictly patri-archal, patrilocal, exogamous and patrilineal. This means that the society is male dominated, normally men bring their wives from other villages into their own childhood home, and inheritance follows the male line, all 'social units, households, are based upon males who are recruited by birth, generation after generation'.[3] One could also define the structure of this society as patricentric in organizational terms, as Denich suggests: 'social structure in which the core residential and economic units consist of agnatically related men'.[4] The social pressure of the *fis* (tribe or clan), all those descended from one male ancestor, also asserts an influence.[5] Rural northern Albania retains much of its patriarchal organization, including large family size and the functions of joint family households. Backer comments that 'the "Albanian tribal society" is usually described as one of the most patriarchal in the world'.[6] The complicated Albanian kinship structure exists within the intricate system of the clans.[7] The head of each *fis* is its hereditary *bajraktar* (standard-bearer).

The British traveller and writer, Edith Durham made a careful study of the clan system and was the first to write in detail in English on the subject.[8] Reineck comments that the term 'tribal people' applied to Albanians is problematic 'due to the diversity of local organization among clans'.[9] Backer notes that there is little agreement on the term in Western sources: 'the brave fieldworkers have not been too concerned about the precise terminology, and those using their material in an attempt to analyse the social organization in question (as for example Whitaker) suffer from this'.[10]

Backer clarifies the Albanian family organization as a 'patriarchal triangle'. Its social elements are:

a. patrilineal descent, b. village exogamy and c. inheritance in the male line . . . (which) . . . produced a social pattern of tightly knit agnatic groups. The males become the subjects in society at large, and in social interaction this results in strict control of the women's movements. The logic in limiting the influence of women was not only a question of personal threat to the power of males. It concerned the existence of the system as such.[11]

The Hierarchy

As remarked on in chapter 1, in many ways northern Albania has more in common with Kosov@, than with the rest of Albania (it was only during the Communist period that they developed in different ways). Both areas were for a time a part of the same *vilayet* (taxation district, later a province)[12] and together sought to free themselves from Ottoman domination, especially in the latter part of the nineteenth century. At that time Shkodër was a centre of intellectual life whose writers[13] interacted constantly with those of Prizren in Kosov@ as well as with those of southern Albania. In both northern Albania and in Kosov@ a form (albeit somewhat different) of the Geg dialect is used, and they have a common kinship system involving very large extended families sharing one house (*shpi*).[14] In this unique preserve of Europe, people lived and held land communally long before the theory of Communism was developed. However, all ownership was held by men, women being considered merely a part of their property. It is this situation which gives such importance to the remarkable, but valid option for a woman to become a man. Stahl stresses the importance of having sons, it 'is essential for life after death, since he is the one who will take care of your soul; and it is always the son who carries on with the life of your household; he also inherits the property, goes to war, defends you, and also avenges you'.[15] These needs can equally all be fulfilled by a 'sworn virgin'.

In these families the larger the size, the greater the family's strength. *Guardian* journalist, Jonathan Steele comments: 'This archaic network of extended families is proving to be western Kosovo's salvation as the tide of refugees flows.'[16] Reineck likens the extended family to a corporate group, holding property in common: 'the group acts as one body in the face of disputes with outsiders, there is a leader who represents the group to other groups (the *zoti i shtëpisë*), all members are to outsiders "jurally equal" and are considered representatives of the group'.[17] Without a recognized male leader, the family can no longer function. In this situation the 'sworn virgin' can be paramount.

The large family size represents a kind of chicken-egg situation as far as the self-sufficiency in agriculture is practised. In Kosov@ (part mountain, part lowlands), agriculture is diversified, where the fertile, relatively flat land allows for both livestock and crop cultivation. In the mountainous areas of northern Albania however, the population relies more on dairy products, especially from goats; crop production can only be on a subsistence scale. In both areas there is a dependence on large families to supply the labour needed to ensure a wide variety of production. At the same time, higher production is needed to satisfy the needs of the whole family. This in turn acts to discourage members from seeking work or education elsewhere. However, with new demands for material goods such as televisions and household equipment, there is a growing tendency for families to seek outside work, to operate as smaller units, thus breaking up the property and necessitating some to work outside as wage earners.

Backer claims to have visited the 'largest family in Europe', residing in a village some twenty kilometers from Isniq (the all-Albanian village outside the town of Dečani in Kosov@, where she did her fieldwork).[18] Backer gives an insight into the working of the *shpie*[19]:

I felt it was an organization quite different from the nuclear family I was used to. For one thing you don't get to know the family – but representatives of it selected according to sex, age and status. Their roles are not presented as 'dad' or 'son', but rather something that could be translated into 'prime minister', 'foreign minister' . . . etc. The position of women was also dealt with . . . his wife and some of the younger of the twenty-three married women of the family were present during the meal, although they did not eat with us. Organizing the members for daily routines like meals was not done by subdividing the group into nuclear

Figure 6. Household head with a typical multi-generational patriarchal family who share one home. A *nuse* (new bride) (whose husband is missing from the picture) at far left, is dressed up for the visitor (the photographer). Ann Christine Eek (Samfoto, Norway): Tregtan, Kukës, 1994

units, but arranging them in groups according to the simple and practical principles of sex and age. Elder men ate on their own.[20]

The Household Head

The hierarchy is headed by the *zot i shtëpies* (or *zoti i shtëpisë* or *zot i shpis*)(head),[21] who holds total control of all aspects of life concerning the family; and each household is headed by a man who is held responsible for the division of wealth and labour, also for any bloodfeud debt. His task is one of balancing carefully the many aspects of communal family life such that the house is highly respected in the eyes of all outsiders, not for any individual accomplishment, but for the sum of the productive contributors. Such a man may now be seen to play an important connecting role between the old society, based on the *Kanun* (see next chapter for details of this Code of Law) and the modern outside world.

The head is likely to be married, the father of several sons still living in the household, with their wives and children and his own unmarried daughters.

Figure 7. 'A multiple household might contain as many as twenty persons, a goodly enough number but only a pale reflexion of past glories. All over north Albania it used to be the custom for brothers, first and even second cousins to live with their wives and children, and probably several aged uncles and aunts and young sisters, under the same roof. Enormous housefuls sometimes resulted. For instance, there were sixty-four people in Gjon Macaj's house in Perlat in about 1900, ninety-five in Isuf Isaku's in Zdrajshë in 1923, and seventy in Lushan Sadrija's in Shalë even more recently.' (Hasluck (1954) *The Unwritten Law of Albania*, p. 29). Ann Christine Eek (Samfoto, Norway): Golaj, 1994

Pouqueville clearly does not consider the duties of the household head very arduous:

His occupation is to maintain his arms, to provide care for his shoes, prepare his cartridges, maintain ammunition for war; and the rest of his time is spent smoking and vegetating . . . The disdainful warrior believed himself to be demeaned by manual labor; he waits for his family to do everything; taciturn, he holds the stick of leadership in his hand; he demands attention, services and help from those who depend on him; and he is never concerned with the details of domestic life except to trade or sell the surplus of produce.[22]

If the household head becomes too old or frail, a new head may be nominated either by the outgoing head or by group decision; the transition could be made gradually over a period of time. All being equal the new head would be the oldest son. However, other attributes are considered, for example administrative ability and knowledge of the customary law. With such families numbering up to as many as 100 and even more persons, it is obvious that this is a very significant position; its prestige is far greater than that of an ordinary man, and not one attained by all men. As a 'sworn virgin' is chosen to head a family when no other suitable male is available, it is likely that such a family is less extensive.

The actions of the headman must be conducted with the good of the household in mind, he should be watchful that the land does not remain uncultivated and that the animals are in good health. He should obtain clothes for his group, be fair and unbiased. If someone wants to enter the house, it is the leader that they call on.

The household head makes decisions for the whole extended family concerning all matters: marriage, education, employment, even the clothing of any of its members. Ian Whitaker further outlines many other duties of the *zot i shpis* including the purchase of a rifle for each youth in the family on reaching the age when he might be involved in a bloodfeud. Amongst other duties, the household head represents the family at village meetings. As such a representative he is elegible, if chosen by the community, to become a village-chief (*kryeplak*).[23] Besides his duties, there are also certain privileges that his status allows him. Margaret Hasluck details some of these:

> The master received no money payments for his services but enjoyed certain privileges. His clothes were often newer and of better cloth than those of his subordinates; more silver chains crossed his breast, and more silver rings glittered on his fingers. He was entitled to have his own bedding and coffee utensils and to keep them until he died. If he chose to buy himself a riding horse, a watch, or arms richly inlaid with silver and bright stones, he might do so. His subordinates, though left to walk while he rode, to learn the time from the sun by day and from the crowing of a cock at night, and to content themselves with the plainest of rifles and revolvers, did not seem to resent his magnificence. He represented the family, and the worthier he appeared in externals as well as in mind and character, the greater the glory reflected on each of them.[24]

'In Albanian society, the so-called Lord of the House is a revered institution, the decision maker for the whole clan.'[25] Reineck explains that above and beyond the position of the Master of the House whose authority is unquestioned, it is the role of the Mistress of the House, as the most senior woman, to direct the domestic work of the other women to conform with the Master's expected running of the house: 'his will extends into every aspect of communal life'. Reineck also notes the importance of the *oda* or main living room which is primarily a male domain:[26] even boys are excluded until they are brought in with a serious understanding of their role as future discussants of family decisions. This is also the room to which male and foreign guests are brought.

Property Ownership and Inheritance

As already pointed out above, property is owned corporately by the family, administered by the household head. During the 1990s, large closely-knit families were still the norm in rural northern Albania and Kosov@; however, there has been a decline in total self-sufficiency. In Kosov@, despite its more fertile land, the increased population, along with partible inheritance, resulted in less land per family. Throughout the 1980s, men were forced to go further afield to find a living, thousands emigrated for years at a time, sending money home to keep the rest of the family together, guarding its property.[27] Vickers comments on the strength of family loyalty and the lengths to which young migrant workers go in order to assist and maintain their traditional families remaining in Kosov@.[28]

In northern Albania, there was no possibility for ordinary people to supplement the family income by migrating during the Communist period as Kosovars could to Germany, Switzerland, the Netherlands and other European countries. Migrant Kosovars were able to earn enough to increase the collective material wealth sufficiently to bring back cars, televisions, washing machines and other goods to raise the living standard in ways which were not possible in Albania itself at that time. Some put their money towards part shares (with other families) in tractors and other items with which to help increase production from their land. This has not been the case in Albania, even since 1990, where the very recent novelty of consumer goods has prioritized televisions and modern household equipment over goods whose immediate satisfaction is not felt. Sometimes such equipment as washing machines stand only as a status symbol in houses without running water and only a rudimentary and erratic electrical system without the power needed for more than a meagre lighting system. While the importance of agriculture slightly declined in Kosov@, it remained the way of life for the majority in northern Albania for another decade.

Patrilineality ensures the principles of male inheritance. The *Kanun* spells out clearly that only sons (from age fifteen) shall inherit. It also details a kinship system whereby relationships through the male side are known as stemming from 'The Tree of Blood' and those through the female side as stemming from 'The Tree of Milk'.[29] If there is no male, 'sworn virgin' or *kollovar* (see below) to take over the household, the property should pass to the closest male relative of the widow. She, along with all the contents would then also become his property.[30] Rose Wilder Lane met a woman who was recently widowed. Her husband had built the two-roomed house in which she had lived with him and their children. Lane found it extraordinary that on his death it was decided that the widow's brother-in-law and a total of sixteen family members should move in with her.[31] Indeed in many cases, inheritance was a strong motive force behind the decision for a woman to become a 'sworn virgin', a choice which had 'less to do with gender identity than a way of circumventing the customary law to preserve a family's patrimony.'[32]

There is another alternative which allows a family with no sons to secure inheritance through a daughter. This is a custom practised more in southern Albania than in the north, whereby the youngest daughter in a family may bring her new husband to her birth home to live. Such a man may be from a family of many sons where he will not be missed there as an inheritor. His own family may prefer not to have to find space for yet another family in their home. This man is known as a *kollovar*, and whilst it resolves the problem of care for the daughter's parents in their old age, the status of the *kollovar* is somewhat diminished by moving into his wife's home.

Backer's concluding hypothesis, with its Marxian emphasis, is that 'in the end it is the availability of land with the ratio of land to labour which is the generating factor of economic and social change, given this particular structure.'[33] This affects Albania even more than Kosov@ (about which she was writing), as almost 100 per cent of land in Albania was taken under Communism; this was never true of Kosov@.

Milk Rights: a Woman's Place

'To be a woman is basically an occupational status, if seen socially . . . to keep the household in a way that the male world runs smoothly without problems'.[34] The *Kanun* is explicit about the purpose of women's lives: 'A woman is known as a sack made to endure as long as she lives in her husband's house. Her parents do not interfere in her affairs, but they bear the responsibility for her and must answer for anything dishonorable that she does.'[35] Men's control of women is also outlined: 'the parents of his . . . wife . . . give him (the groom) a cartridge' as protection against 'two acts (for which) a woman may be shot in the back . . . a) for adultery; b) for betrayal of hospitality' (to any guest). The preservation of this law continued to be demonstrated until quite recent times, the bridegroom's parents giving the groom a cartridge on the wedding day.[36]

Despite the very low status of women in rural Albania, the men who live

Figure 8. 'Grues mos i shif hundet, po punet.' (Do not judge a woman by her looks, but by her work). Traditional Albanian proverb. Kirsten Senturia White: 1994

by the laws of the *Kanun* consider that women are well looked after and highly respected. They point out that should anyone outside the family dishonour a woman, such offence would be considered a shameful attack, and appropriate action would be taken. However, it is the family's honour rather than that of the woman herself which is at stake: a matter which could possibly result in blood vengeance. A woman is the possession first of her father's household, and on marriage, of her husband's, in whose family she remains the most inferior person until she bears a son. 'For a man to obtain a wife, she must be directly or indirectly given to him by another man who, in the simplest case is posited as father or brother.'[37] Despite questioning the universality of Lévi-Strauss's theory of 'woman-exchange', Denich considers it to be a useful model for kinship structures in the Balkans: 'the exchange of women leads to the formation of male groups, not groups acknowledging the equal participation of both sexes'.[38]

Backer also points out that due to peculiarities connected with the indirect dowry and patrilineal social organization, there have been some misconceptions about the way Albanian women are treated. Such phrases are used as 'The Albanians sell their women', 'The Albanians may shoot their women if they please', and 'Among the Albanians a woman is worth less than a donkey'.[39] These stereotypes may be based on real situations, including the use of bride-price, but need to be contextualized. However, within the *Kanun* an act of domestic violence, where deemed 'appropriate', is seen as a form of social justice.

Betrothal: Arranged Marriage

David Gilmore comments that 'One specific domain of Mediterranean culture that seems to provide solid analytical analogies, despite some formal diversity, is that of male-female relations . . . the Mediterranean value system . . . and associated issues of chastity and virginity.'[40]

Courtship or dating are still unknown concepts in rural Albania amongst young people who have always been kept segregated from an early age. According to tradition, it is expected that a couple should not meet before their marriage. Usually girls are curious to know what their future husband looks like, but it is considered shameful to show an interest. Backer explains that if a man possessed a photograph of his fiancé it could be taken as proof that he was having an illicit relationship with her, for which she in particular would receive extreme and lifelong condemnation.[41] This in turn would reflect very badly not only on the girl, but on her entire family. In the rural areas there is little opportunity for socializing in mixed groups, much less to form relationships of a sexual nature. Girls have to stay at home and are constantly employed with household chores and carrying firewood and water. They have little interaction outside the home, and even now are sometimes prevented from attending school. Boys, with no household duties, are free to meet friends and leave their homes unrestricted. Men do no work in the house and are served, even having their feet washed by women.[42] Fisher notes Hibbert's point that in the partisan forces, where females comprised 9 per cent, fraternalization between the sexes was severely punishable.[43]

Backer comments on the fact that love was seen as a weakness of women and this is the justification for the need of their protection. On the other hand, although it was assumed that men naturally had sexual desires, they were not considered real men if they demonstrated interest in women: 'A man who either was very attractive to women and a flirt, or who fell in love, was more or less considered a weak man. He was not really reliable, often called a "fool" and considered a vain person not being able to control himself properly' for 'love was the unfortunate inclination of the young and inexperienced and was definitely not expected to decide the future of a household . . . love and marriage existed apart from each other.'[44] This point was confirmed to me in all my interviews with 'sworn virgins', less by what they said than by their very disinterest in the matter.

Figure 9. A Bektashi *sheh* and his very young bride (it was *he* who insisted on the
roses). Ann Christine Eek (Samfoto, Norway), at a *teke* outside Kukës,
1994

Traditionally the new bride receives little comfort from her husband, for
she should not be seen communicating in any way with him; if it is essential,
she should do so in whispers. Hasluck reports this as the normal practise.[45]

Susan Pritchett Post provides ethnographical material from earlier decades,
by interviewing older women, for example 'Shyqyri's Story' tells not only
Shyqyri's role, but the whole family structure already outlined:

> ... a marriage was arranged for me when I was thirteen years of age to a man
> who was twenty-two years older than I ... I had not yet reached puberty and
> could not yet sleep with my husband ... for two years ...
> My husband helped me to grow up, but he beat me when I played with other
> girls my own age ... He told me not to raise my head up while walking to the
> field or going to the mountain to cut wood. I had to look down and fix my gaze
> on the tips of my shoes ... Ours was a typical patriarchal family. We (the women
> of the family) never had the right to speak to our husbands in front of others. It
> was considered to be shameful to do that. The women in our house never entered
> a room where the men were gathered to talk, drink coffee, or eat lunch. It was the
> duty of the women to prepare and bring coffee, food, etc., to the room – to the
> door of the room. We had to work and bear children.

When I joined the family there were twenty people in the house . . . I gave birth to
a total of eleven children . . . the first eight were born one and a half years apart . . .
When I was pregnant I had to keep my pregnancy secret from the people in the
house and from my husband . . . It was considered shameful to be pregnant. I . . .
returned to work just three days after the birth of each child . . .
When our daughters grew up and the time to marry them came, only my husband
had the right to decide on such a problem. I was not asked at all to give my
opinion about my daughter's marriage.[46]

The above still holds true to this day in many rural areas in northern Albania,
and relates equally to 'sworn virgins' as decision-makers. In other parts of
Albania, mixed-group social activities are acceptable amongst students, but
even these are usually only amongst known and respected colleagues. Robert
Carver portrays a similar picture of a woman in Radomire.[47] In the 1990s,
Tirana has become an exception, where Westernized families are rapidly
changing their values.

The traditions of patrilocality ensure that a young bride marries outside
her own village and moves into the home of her husband's family. Marriages
may be arranged by parents as early as the time of birth or even before. It is
an old practise that men may exchange children or sisters as a token of their
friendship.[48] Traditionally a bride-price is negotiated by families and paid by
the groom's family. This may be in two instalments, the first upon agreement
of the price, the second at the time of the marriage.[49] There is therefore
continual interest maintained in both the bride's good upbringing and the
constant preservation of her purity.

The value of the girl traditionally lay in her purity and her willingness and
ability to work hard. Durham enquired about bride-price wherever she went,
and found that it varied considerably by area. In many places there was a
general agreement that it would not exceed a certain sum. She commented on
the fact that in Pulati and Dukagjin the bride-price was lower than elsewhere,
and that an elderly widow might change hands for a rifle![50]

In cases where marriage partners have not been selected in early childhood,
parents have very different criteria depending on whether they are choosing a
son-in-law or a daughter-in-law. Backer's informant explained:

'When we are evaluating a prospective son-in-law, first we look at his personality,
then his family. But when a daughter-in-law is selected, the whole family on both
sides is examined first, then the girl'. There is a stress on the family of the wife,
compared to that of an outmarried sister.[51]

As a girl's family needs to be sure that she is worthy of her bride-price and
acceptable to the family she will marry into, they need to restrict any possible

Figure 10. It is usual for women to perform two, three or even more tasks all at the same time. This woman has collected water and will continue spinning wool as she takes the bottle home. AY: Boga, 1993

slur on her character. Even today in Albania, girls' schooling and activities may be severely curtailed in order to ensure their good reputations. Although Post found that some teenagers were breaking from the old norms of arranged marriages by marrying for love, still many families keep their teenage girls away from secondary school believing it 'is a place for love stories'. She interviewed Ina, a teenage girl who told her:

Figure 11. The bride is presented to the women from the bridegroom's family who have just arrived to bring her to her new home. The reception for the groom and the men of both families are in another house. Ann Christine Eek (Samfoto, Norway), Junik, Kosov@, 1976

I have led a quiet life . . . when I was young, I competed for ballet. I didn't win and that was a shock, but what came after was the real shock. I wanted to go on dancing, but couldn't. Why? Because all the village gossiped about me. They called me a 'bad' girl. Even the children in school brought this opinion of me from home. When I was only twelve I received a letter accusing me of being a prostitute. I wanted to make up for this opinion so for three years I stayed closed up and away from others.[52]

Similarly, other teenagers whom Post interviewed were prevented by their parents from attending secondary school or university for fear that they might be injured, raped or simply fall in love and marry someone without regard to traditional arrangements. In some areas girls are permitted to work in the fields outside the home, but in others young girls, those engaged and even the young married women are kept within the family compound, away from the possible sight of men.

Beyond the Wedding Day

From the day of her marriage her husband's name (in the possessive form) is used when speaking of her. Backer confirms the maintenance of this control:

Figure 12. Bride at her wedding reception. Never having met her husband before
their wedding day, the bride may well be nervous of the new life that
awaits her amidst a family she does not know. AY: Okolo, 1993

'adultery was punished most severely with the right of the offended male be it
father, brother or husband to kill both woman and lover'.[53]

The wedding celebrates the links between two families and their respect for
one another, rather than the union of two people. The bride is the energetic
young addition to the workforce, potential bearer of future inheritors to the
home and land. She is the only person who does not share in the celebrations
following the wedding ceremony. She stands, eyes downcast while all the
guests partake of the lavish quantities of food and drink. Several observers
have described her plight; Rose Wilder Lane wrote:

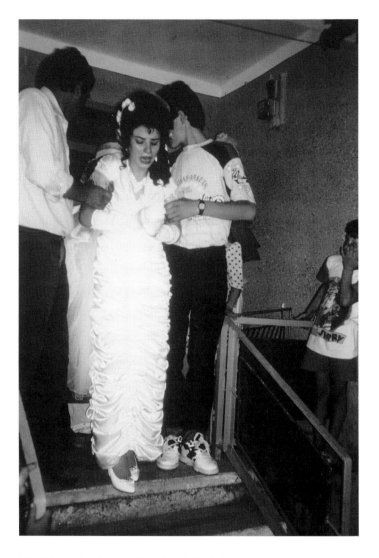

Figure 13. Bride being fetched from her father's home. It is normal for the bride to shed demonstrative tears on this occasion when she is leaving her birth family. AY: outside Shkodër, 1994

When the bride arrives at her husband's house she takes a humble place in the corner, standing, her hands folded on her breast, her eyes downcast, and for three days and nights she is required to remain in that position, without lifting her eyes, without moving, and without eating or drinking. On the second day . . . she goes about the household, obeying the commands of the elders, always standing until they tell her to sit, and for six months, not speaking unless they address her.[54]

Janet Reineck describes the situation more vividly:

> In a high mountain village it is the morning after a wedding. A rooster crows. It must be day, but still dark. And cold. December. Her eyes sting, her head aches from too little sleep, from the cold. She isn't groggy. She wakes into a chilling awareness of her new life, and her new name, 'Bride'. The awareness stings her, rushes her pulse. The awareness, the sting, will hit her, wrench her from sleep, day after day, for months, for years, gradually diminishing, becoming ritual, habit, as she molds herself to fit her new persona.[55]

When she goes to her new husband's home she is known as *nuse* (new bride) until another son marries. During the first month of marriage a new bride is expected to be dressed in her best clothing and be ready at any time for visitors coming to meet her to approve her as a worthy new addition to the household.

Many of the women whom Post interviewed, described their arranged marriages, and accepted them as the norm. Even when their situations seem far from ideal, women manage to accept them with resignation.[56] However, one woman in particular describes the difficult life she has had as a result of her marriage:

> My parents were extremely conservative . . . they would not allow me to finish high school because they were worried that I would be subjected to sexual abuse . . . I worked only a short time because my parents arranged a marriage for me.
> I was engaged and married quickly, knowing nothing of my husband or his family. It was worse than I expected it to be and I have had to face all kinds of hardships alone . . . Although my husband has treated me badly, I couldn't consider divorce because of the social consequences I would suffer. I don't feel that I am unusual because most of the Albanian women are under the dictatorship of their husbands.[57]

The ritual sobbing of a bride at leaving her parents' home signifies her own loss of identity. It may well be a sad day for her as she leaves the familiarity of her own extended family which she is likely never to have left before. The young couple probably meet for the first time on their wedding day.

The new family is a cohesive group who remain in the bridegroom's home. Through the practise of exogamy, daughters born into the family cannot expect to spend their adulthood with those with whom they are familiar. The wives brought into the home are likely to be strangers to one another, though they must learn their hierarchical place and work together under the direction of the wife of the head of the household. Women do visit their blood family at times. The frequency depends not only on the distance between families, but also on the attitude of the new family to the woman's absence – or rather the absence of her labour. Since marriage is exogamous and transport invariably on foot, such visits require time and effort to achieve. A woman is likely to take her small children with her on such visits, but none whose productive work would be missed as the visit can extend to as long as a month at a time.

It is taken for granted that women marry and have children. Carver met a middle-aged woman who was in the unusual position of not having married; he describes her attempts to present her domestic situation to fit the normal servile mould:

> Angeliki 'has had the misfortune never to be married . . .' Gabriel had told me seriously. Not to be married, not to have children in Albania was regarded as a catastrophe. Angeliki's brother and his family were away . . . Angeliki was alone in the family house.
> The arrangement was that I would pay $10 a day, without food; but Angeliki was an old-fashioned Albanian lady, and having a man in the house was an excuse for her to cook, and cook and cook . . .
> Angeliki had no pretensions at all to being either modern or Western. I was a man, the man of the house, in the absence of any other. Everything thus centred around my comfort and gastronomic demands.
> She managed to round up three of her young nieces and a nephew, who were brought in to complete the ersatz family circle. Thus I would be seated at the head of the table, while the oldest niece, perhaps five years old, solemnly served me raki . . . The nieces and nephew chattered on to Angeliki in Albanian, while I smiled on, a vicarious, mute patriarch.
> This was as close as Angeliki would ever get to being married.[58]

The preference for boy babies is a worldwide phenomenon. In some societies men take second and even third wives if a first one does not produce a son.[59] Jelka Vince-Pallua notes 'the wife's most important function is to bear heirs for the male line . . . some Montenegrins do not count daughters, and when they are asked how many children they have, they only mention the number of sons, or they say: "Two boys and, if you'll pardon me for saying, three girls!"' This preference did not change in the new Albanian society: mothers still needed consolation at the birth of a daughter.[60] By producing a son a *nuse* gains status: though even then her son is considered to belong to the family while she remains an outsider. Valentini spoke of a man who believed there was no way to be allowed entry into Heaven without a son, essential for life after death in order to take care of the deceased's soul.[61] Sterility, or the inability of a couple to produce sons, is believed to be the woman's fault, in either case she may be sent back to her family and a second wife or even a third one can be taken to replace her.[62] Durham found that in some cases a formal marriage did not even take place until a son was born.[63]

To offset the difficulties and hardships of mothers, those who bear sons gain not only status, but also a very close bond with their sons. Traditionally a son's love for his mother is considered a duty; its demonstration is laudable. Backer notes that 'when sons come of age, they are the ones to protect their mother who has defended them while young. A man admits to crying upon a mother's death, but not on that of his wife.'[64] The son in turn deserves respect from his mother comparable to that she shows to her husband. Men also have close relationships with their sisters, often defending them from unfair decisions made by the rest of the family, or, in recent years, helping them financially towards getting an education. A mother may also find great comfort from her daughters until marriage takes their loyalty to a different household.

It remains true that considerable sexual repression exists especially in traditional rural society. Sex is not discussed or even acknowledged amongst most women and extra-marital sex is theoretically non-existent, rare and severely punishable. Sex for women has always been seen to serve purely a procreative function. Birth control remains little known and undesired, large families are the norm, and the hope of always one more son is reason enough not to seek ways of preventing conception.

Childrearing is a communal responsibility. Girls are trained from early childhood as homecleaners and caterers, while boys are allowed the freedom to play outside the home. These traditions survived through the Communist changes more firmly in the north than elsewhere. Post's interviewee, Fitore, voices this:

> My parents taught me to be honest, frank, and sincere, to have respect for others and to be hospitable. Since they were from the northern part of Albania, hospitality was part of their personality . . . I remember my mother primarily as working, washing, and keeping house. She didn't have much education, but she was well-respected and managed her family well.[65]

Fitore, however, mentions that there were many books in her home and she was encouraged to read.

Carver describes his observation of sex role differentiation amongst some children:

> I was able to watch the Frasheris' grandchildren at play in the garden as I sat and ate cherries with their grandfather. They had no toys at all, and their game always revolved around the older boys chasing, catching and beating the younger boys, while the girls watched; then the younger boys escaping and in turn chasing the girls, catching them and then beating them and making them squeal . . . None of the adults interfered or mediated in these exchanges . . . This catch-and-beat play was confined to the garden. Girls never chased or beat, but were purely passive.

Once in the house this play ceased, and the girls had to wait upon the adult males as they were bidden, while the boys were cossetted and fondled by their female adult relatives. Girls were never cossetted or fondled by either adult males or females; their role was to wait upon the men inside the house, and to be chased and beaten in the garden. Beyond the garden the girls were not allowed to go, though the boys could play in the lane outside.[66]

Even more recently Dr. Michael Ruttenberg, working with Kosovar refugees in the Stenkovic camp in Macedonia, noted that 'There was a swimming hole for the kids (but no girls swimming) . . . no girls . . . Only boys.'[67]

The Death of a Husband

'Levirate', the practise of a widow automatically being married to her dead husband's brother or even cousin or uncle, is still observed on occasion to this day. The widow may find no way to avoid the situation as she is not free to leave the family who have paid her bride-price, without their permission. More than one such case has come to the notice of immigration authorities in Canada and the United States, where the widow has managed to escape by seeking asylum in order to avoid what in Canada is deemed to be 'forced marriage'.[68]

Division of Labour

The *Kanun* gives a detailed description of the rigidly gendered division of labour by which people live in the northern Albanian Alps. Traditional men's work, and exactly the same applies for 'sworn virgins', includes all heavy manual work: ploughing, hoeing, harrowing, manure spreading, chopping wood, scything, mowing, harvesting, watering and maintaining irrigation systems, protecting animals and property; it also includes being a host: talking to visitors, drinking and smoking with them, and avenging family honour (this last task is of extreme importance, taking precedence over all others, as discussed at some length in Chapter 5). The more specific tasks of household heads, as the family decision-makers, has already been discussed (p. 18). All men are included in the negotiations upon which the family head will make the final decision. Women on the other hand are privy to none of them, and will only know of changed plans, even ones which affect their whole lives, once the decision has been made.[69]

Women's tasks include conceiving, bearing and rearing children, baking bread, cooking and house cleaning, tending the outside earth-closets, serving

Figure 14. Women at work at the communal village water source, constantly busy but never overcrowded. All day long there was a steady stream of women and children collecting pure mountain water, doing washing and watering animals. As Campbell notes ((1964), *Honour, Family and Patronage*): 'men never carry burdens on their backs. However sick or feeble his wife or daughter, a man will never help her with the intolerable burden of heavy water barrels.' Note contrasts of traditional and more modern clothing and of wooden and plastic water containers. All the women, whether in traditonal or more modern attire, wear skirts. AY: Boga, 1993

the men and guests (including washing their feet), carrying water and firewood, tending fires and poultry, attending to dairy production and taking it to market, storing and processing food, processing and weaving wool, washing and mending clothes, manufacturing garments for the family, for trousseaux and for sale, embroidering garments and linen. All these tasks are performed without running water. Additionally they must assist men at times of particular harvesting, collecting and transporting the produce, and at times the older women may be expected to help milk the sheep in their summer pastures. Women may also be seen spinning or knitting at the same time as performing several of the above tasks.

Backer calculates that women provide as much as 60 per cent of the work of men in agricultural primary production, besides performing all the domestic

Figure 15. The wooden water casket keeps the water cooler than plastic
containers. Some women have to carry the family's water several miles.
AY: Boga, 1993

and childcare work within the house,[70] but 'the household chores of women
are not really considered as work'.[71] Furthermore, women may be called
upon to take over completely the men's outdoor tasks in times of war, or feud
when it is unsafe for the men to venture out of the house.

J.K. Campbell's study of institutions and moral values in a Greek mountain community apply equally to the northern Albanian case: 'clearly manliness and shame are complementary qualities in relation to honour. The manliness of the men in any family protects the sexual honour of its women from external insult or outrage. The women must have shame if the manliness of the men is not to be dishonoured.'[72]

Notes

1. Article CII in Gejçov, S. (1989), *Kanuni i Lekë Dukagjinit* (The Code of Lek Dukagjini), translated by L. Fox, New York: Gjonlekaj Publishing Co. See also Donert, C.: 'The trees of blood and milk referred to in the *Kanun* metaphorically represent the fact that '"'a man has blood, and a woman kin', i.e., a man has a pedigree, and a woman has her own relatives, and 'a woman is anybody's daughter,' i.e., comes from anywhere and has no pedigree"' (quoted from Hasluck (1954), *The Unwritten Law in Albania*, (1999), 'Trees of Blood and Trees of Milk: Customary Law and the Construction of Gender in Albania', MA thesis, Albanian Studies, School of Slavonic and East European Studies, London University, p. 7.

2. Goldsworthy, V. (1998), *Inventing Ruritania: the Imperialism of the Imagination*, New Haven; London: Yale University Press, p. 200.

3. Denich, B.S. (1974), 'Sex and Power in the Balkans' in Rosaldo, M.Z. and Lamphere, L. (eds), *Woman, Culture and Society*, Stanford, California: Stanford University Press, p. 244.

4. Denich (1974), 'Sex and Power in the Balkans'.

5. For discussion on tribes in Albania, see Durham (1928), *Some Tribal Origins, Laws and Customs of the Balkans*, London: Allen & Unwin, pp. 13–58.

6. Backer, B. (1979), *Behind the Stone Walls: Changing Household Organization among the Albanians of Kosovo*, Oslo: PRIO-publications S-8/79, p. 142.

7. The twelve original Geg clans are: Berisha, Bytyçi, Gashi, Gruda, Hoti, Kelmendi, Krasniqi, Kuçi, Merturi, Shala, Shoshi and Thaç, which each lived in their own areas throughout northern Albania and Kosov@.

8. She wrote in a form which is accessible not only to specialists. She claims that the ancestors of the Albanians, the Illyrians were absorbed by the 'inrushing Slav', and that they 'professed Christianity for some fifteen centuries'; see Durham, M. E. (1909, 1985, 1987), *High Albania*, London: Edward Arnold. Republished and edited by John Hodgson, London: Virago, Boston: Beacon Press, pp. 4, 21.

9. Reineck, J. (1991), *The Past as Refuge: Gender, Migration and Ideology among the Kosova Albanians*, Ph.D thesis, University of California at Berkeley, p. 42.

10. Backer (1979), *Behind the Stone Walls*, p. 92.

11. Backer (1979), *Behind the Stone Walls*, pp. 169–70.

12. The exact size and shape of the *vilayets* varied as power was differently exerted.

Present-day boundaries do not exactly co-incide with earlier ones which bordered areas of the same name. See Malcolm, N. (1998), *Kosovo: a Short History*, London: Macmillan, pp. 191–2.

13. For example the Frashëri brothers: Abdyl (1839–92), Naim (1846–1900) and Sami (1850–1904). Abdyl was the most influential member of the League of Prizren (founded in 1878), he was imprisoned for his political activities. Naim and Sami were prolific writers on matters of Albanian national awakening. Naim published work concerning the emancipation of women and universal education. Sami devised an Albanian alphabet (at a time when there was no standard Albanian alphabet) which was accepted by the alphabet Committee of 1879, though later banned under Ottoman rule.

14. The term *shtëpie*, originating from the Tosk dialect of the South, is that incorporated into the standardized language (Unified Literary Albanian or ULA) approved in 1972. The more commonly known term anthropologically is *zadruga*, the Serbo-Croatian name. This is probably due to the fact that until 1991 it was only possible for Western anthropologists to study the phenomenon in Yugoslavia, where these large families were common both amongst Serbs and Albanians; however the language used for research is likely to have been Serbo-Croatian rather than Albanian, even in Kosov@, because permission to conduct the research would have to be sought through the Serb capital, Belgrade. See for example Erlich, V. (1976), 'The Last Big *Zadrugas*: Albanian Extended Families in the Kosovo Region' in Byrnes, R.F. (ed.) (1976), *Communal Families in the Balkans: the 'Zadruga': Essays by Philip E. Mosely and Essays in his Honor*, Notre Dame, Indiana: University of Notre Dame Press, pp. 244–5l; and Halpern, J.M. and Anderson, D. (1970), 'The *Zadruga*: a Century of Change' *Anthropologica*, vol. 12.

15. Stahl, P.H. (1986) 'The Albanians' (ch. III) *Household, Village and Village Confederation in Southeastern Europe*, Boulder, Colorado: East European Monographs (no. 200), p. 107.

16. Steele, J. (8 June 1998), 'We Must Rescue the Oppressed of Kosovo. And here's how to do it', in *The Guardian*.

17. Reineck (1991), *The Past as Refuge*, p. 55.

18. Ann Christine Eek (photographer) who worked with Backer, reports on Isniq following attacks by the Yugoslav Army which started in 1998. On 4 and 5 April 1999 the people (mostly women and children, many men had already left) were forced to leave their homes, which were then plundered. Their identity papers were confiscated and they were sent off on tractors towards Albania. Before they reached nearby Dečani, they saw their houses burning.

19. Reineck uses the form *shtëpia*. I have found considerable disagreement over the exact spelling and use of this word, but quote from correspondence with the writer and translator, Robert Elsie (17 April 1999): 'It simply depends how you look at it. Standard Albanian has *stëpi* whereas Gheg dialect (including formerly, literature in Gheg) uses *shpi*. *Shpi* is also the spoken form heard throughout northern and central Albania, including Tirana. Someone from Tirana would perhaps write *shtëpi* but would say *shpi*. The connection to education lies in the fact that an

educated speaker would endeavour to speak standard Albanian. He would thus say *shtëpi*, though he might then use *shpi* when talking to his grandmother.

20. Backer (1979), *Behind the Stone Walls*, p. 12.

21. Edith Durham calls him the *xot i shpis*.

22. Pouqueville, F.-C.-H.-L. (1826), *Travels in Epirus, Albania, Macedonia and Thessaly*, London: Richard Phillips, III, p. 272, quoted in Stahl (1986), 'The Albanians,' p. 95.

23. Whitaker, I. (1981), 'A Sack for Carrying Things: the Traditional Role of Women in Northern Albanian Society' in *Anthropological Quarterly*, vol. 54, no. 3, p. 197.

24. Hasluck, M. (1954), *The Unwritten Law in Albania*, Cambridge: Cambridge University Press, p. 39.

25. Kusovac, Z. (Sept. 1998), 'Round Two: Serbian Security Forces: The Kosovo Liberation Army is Down but not Out', *Transitions*, vol. 5, no. 9, p. 23.

26. In houses which I visited, this was the room to which I was usually taken on first visits. Guests have to become very familiar friends to be easily accepted into any other rooms.

27. Backer estimated that Kosovar Albanian unskilled migrant workers in Germany were able to save DM 1,000 per month (in the mid-1970s); see Backer (1979), *Behind the Stone Walls*, p. 223.

28. Vickers, M. (1998), *Between Serb and Albanian: a History of Kosovo*, London: Hurst & Co., p. 176.

29. Article CII in Gjeçov (1989), *Kanuni i Lekë Dukagjinit*, p. 142.

30. Gjeçov (1989), *Kanuni i Lekë Dukagjinit*, articles 88, 95, 98, p. 52.

31. Lane, R.W. (1922) *The Peaks of Shala: Being a Record of Certain Wanderings among the Hill-Tribes of Albania*, London: Chapman & Dodd; New York: Harper & Bros., p. 107.

32. Donert, C. (1999), *Trees of Blood and Trees of Milk: Customary Law and the Construction of Gender in Albania*, MA thesis, Albanian Studies, School for Slavonic and East European Studies, University of London.

33. Backer, (1979), *Behind the Stone Walls*, p. 127.

34. Backer (1979), *Behind the Stone Walls*, p. 307.

35. Article XXIX of the *Kanun*: Gjeçov (1989), *Kanuni i Lekë Dukagjinit*, p. 38.

36. Gjeçov (1989), *Kanuni i Lekë Dukagjinit*, Article XXXI, p. 40.

37. Lévi-Strauss, C. (1978), *Structural Anthropology*, London: Penguin Books, p. 83.

38. Denich, (1974), 'Sex and Power in the Balkans', p. 246.

39. Backer (1979), *Behind the Stone Walls*, p. 311.

40. Gilmore, D. (Dec. 1985), 'Introduction' Special Issue no. 3, Gilmore, D. and Gwynne, G. (eds) 'Sex and Gender in Southern Europe: Problems and Prospects', *Anthropology*, vol. 9, now. 1 and 2, p. 1.

41. Backer (1979), *Behind the Stone Walls*, p. 306.

42. A service performed to this day as several foreign writers have observed and personally undergone (in their guest status) this author included.

43. Fischer, B.J. (1999), *Albania at War, 1539–1945*, London: Hirst, p. 207, quoted in Hibbert, R. (1991), *Albania's National Liberation Struggle: the Bitter Victory*, London: Pinter, New York: St Martin's Press, p. 146.

44. Backer (1979), *Behind the Stone Walls*, p. 303.

45. Hasluck, M. (1954), *The Unwritten Law in Albania*, p. 31.

46. Post, S.E.P. (1988), *Women in Modern Albania*, Jefferson, North Carolina; London: McFarland, pp. 62–3.

47. Carver, R. (1998), *The Accursed Mountains: Journeys in Albania*, London: John Murray, p. 214.

48. Backer (1979), *Behind the Stone Walls*, p. 153.

49. See Hasluck, M. and Myres, J.L. (Dec. 1933), 'Bride Price in Albania: A Homeric Parallel', *Man*, vol. 3, nos. 202–3, pp. 191–6.

50. Durham, M.E. (1928), *Some Tribal Origins, Laws and Customs of the Balkans*, London: Allen & Unwin, p. 192.

51. Backer (1979), *Behind Stone Walls*, p. 141.

52. Post (1998), *Women in Modern Albania*, p. 236.

53. Backer (1979), *Behind the Stone Walls*, p. 171.

54. Lane (1922), *The Peaks of Shala*, p. 25.

55. Reineck (1991), *The Past as Refuge*, p. 9.

56. Backer explains that the term *të pajtuar* (which can be translated as 'adapt') is frequently used by women who grow to accept the new marital environment. The term can also mean to 'reach peace' in the sense that a conflict is solved, followed by resignation. Backer, B. (1981–5) ms. 'Living and Working in Albania' (permission of A.C. Eek, Oslo), p. 26.

57. Post (1998), *Women in Modern Albania*, p. 143.

58. Carver (1998), *The Accursed Mountains*, pp. 90–2.

59. Vince-Pallua, J. (1996), 'Introducing a Second Wife: a Matrimonial Aid in Cases of a Childless Marriage', *International Journal of Anthropology*, vol. 11, no. 1, p. 37. See also Tirta, M. (11 June 1999), 'The Cult of Several Ancient Customs in the Albanian Ethnical Survival' paper delivered to the conference 'Myths in the Politics of Transition', Albanian Studies, School of Slavonic and East European Studies, University of London, p. 6.

60. Susan Pritchett Post explains the Albanian proverb 'when a girl was born the very beams of the house began crying': the parents would be sad because a daughter's dowry would be expensive, an unproductive use of money, and the mother would frequently grieve for the difficult life that lay ahead for her daughter; Post (1998), *Women in Modern Albania*, p. 133.

61. Quoted by Stahl (1986) in 'The Albanians', p. 107.

62. See Stahl (1986), 'The Albanians', p. 108; and Durham (1928), *Some Tribal Origins*, p. 73.

63. Durham, M.E. (1910), 'High Albania and its Customs in 1908', *Journal of the Royal Anthropological Institute of Great Britain and Ireland*, no. 40, p. 459.

64. Backer (1979), *Behind the Stone Walls*, p. 143.

65. Post (1998), *Women of Modern Albania*, p. 142.

66. Carver (1998), *The Accursed Mountains*, pp. 210–11.

67. Coleman, K. (4 June 1999), 'The Good Doctor', *Express* (East Bay, California), vol. 21, no. 35, p. 10.

68. The author's expertise was sought to support such a claim in Canada in 1997.

69. Backer (1979), *Behind the Stone Walls*, p. 288.

70. Backer (1979), *Behind the Stone Walls*, p. 199.

71. See Post's summary of this and on other women's lives in this period: Post (1998), *Women in Modern Albania*, p. 152.

72. Campbell, J.K. (1964, 74), *Honour, Family and Patronage*, Oxford; New York: Oxford University Press, p. 271.

3

The 'Kanun': Laws of Honour and Hospitality

'A man who has been dishonoured is considered dead according to the *Kanun*.'

Article 600 of the *Kanun*.[1]

The *Kanun*

Many of northern Albania's people still live by the strict laws of the *Kanun* whose 1,262 Articles, set out in the twelve 'books' cover all aspects of mountain life: the regulation of economic and family organization, hospitality, brotherhood, the clan, boundaries, work, marriage, land and livestock, etc. The first section of 'Book eight' sets out the laws pertaining to 'Personal Honour' where there is said to be no distinction between man and man, 'Soul for soul, all are equal before God'.[2] The nine articles dealing with personal honour include one which specifies that 'An offense to honor is not paid for with property, but by the spilling of blood or by a magnanimous pardon (through the mediation of good friends).'[3] As already mentioned, both the 'spilling of blood' (of men only) and the need to maintain family honour by having a revered household head, are particularly pertinent to understanding why the 'sworn virgin' emerged in Albanian agrarian society.

Comprehension of the strict adherence to the *Kanun* (discussed in more detail in Appendix 1) is necessary to understanding how 'sworn virgins' fit so crucially within the society which follows this body of law, developed over several centuries. The Albanian people have traditionally lived an ordered life without resort to outside jurisdiction; this differs markedly from anything that exists elsewhere in Europe. One of the *Kanun*'s most positive aspects is its concern for the common good.[4] Although the laws were in operation long before the mass conversion to Islam in the seventeenth century, those already living under the laws of the *Kanun* allowed their religion to be subordinated to it.

There are several quite similar versions of the *Kanun* laws of Albania, the best known and most generally followed to this day is the *Kanun* of Lek Dukagjini. However reference in this *Kanun* to 'sworn virgins' is very brief,[5] whereas there is much more extensive discussion of *virgjinesha* (sworn virgins) in the *Kanun* of Skanderbeg.[6] Here it is stated that they should sit (as does the household head) in the most honoured place both beside the hearth and at the *sofra* (low table on which meals are served to those sitting on the floor).[7] The reasons for becoming a 'sworn virgin' and conditions are also stated in this *Kanun*.[8] This version of the *Kanun* even allows for a woman to take the vow purely by her own choice, even if the conditions giving rise to the need are not present. However, it continues, since the oath is binding for life; in these cases she must first get the permission of her parents and relatives who will be likely to ask her to postpone the change, giving time to give it full consideration in order to be certain that the family will not be shamed by her possible later change of heart.[9] The *Kanun* of Skanderbeg applied to a geographical area where customary laws have since to a large extent lost their following.

The Power of the *Besa*

The *besa* (oath or binding promise) is of prime importance, the cornerstone of all personal and social conduct. Two sections of the *Kanun* are devoted to the *besa*. Articles 529–692 of the *Kanun* concern the various aspects of the oath which is considered 'the end of all controversy'. As 'the oath is a religious utterance', whoever uses it is considered legally bound by it. Article 589 cites the punishment for one who has sworn falsely: 'the mark of dishonor remains on his family until the seventh generation'. These laws are the basis of morality which deeply affects Albanians in all their behaviour. Usually a *besa* is considered to be a lifelong promise, as with the 'sworn virgins' (hence the use of the term 'sworn') .

Breaking the Vow

The *besa* confirms the high value of honour in Albanian society. Combined with extreme social pressure to abide by vows taken, it is exceptional for a 'sworn virgin' to break her vow and thus dishonour herself and her family line. Once the decision is made by herself or her parents, usually accompanied by a vow of chastity and refusal ever to marry, social pressures ensure that the change is not reversed. The advantages of 'sworn virgin' status are that most become and remain heads of their own families and owners of their birth homes. It is a role often taken from birth or early childhood. A woman's alternative as a 'sworn virgin' allows her to carry on the name and inheritance 'to prevent the house, the hearth and the candle from being extinguished'. Backer comments that 'The general stress in the ... culture is upon the submission of the individual to the culturally defined code of behaviour.'[10]

Whitaker draws attention to the one instance where Edith Durham reported a 'sworn virgin' breaking her oath:[11] 'This action must almost certainly have given rise to a blood-feud between either her own clan, or that of her subsequent husband, and the clan of her rejected fiancé, as the insult would be public.'[12] Consequently, apart from the society-wide importance of honour, to break the vow of celibacy once the oath had been taken would put the 'sworn virgin' and her family at severe risk of retribution.

Jan and Cora Gordon tried to determine the outcome of one who might wish to change her mind after taking the oath. They describe their meeting with a 'sworn virgin' during their travels in Albania in the late 1920s:

Looking closer, we began to doubt the sex of this person ...
'That girl ... has vowed never to marry, so she dresses like a man and does man's work.'
'But if she breaks her vow,' we said, 'does her family pursue her to kill her?'
'She doesn't ever break her vow ... she would be ashamed to. And, anyway, no man would want her any more than he would want his sister ...'
Yet we repeated our questions, 'If? If? If?' we insisted.
'She would have to leave the clan then ... she would be disgraced for ever.'
'But they would not kill her?' we asked.
'Oh, no. She can marry if she likes, but she would not want to. You understand ... she has *sworn* she won't.'[13]

The Hearth: the Heart of the Household

The *oda* (men's room – traditionally reserved for men's discussions and entertaining visitors), where they are served their meals, is also the room to which visitors are taken. Robert Pichler comments on the importance of this room: 'it is striking that the most frequented public place was inside the house, namely the guest-room.'[14] The hearth is the central focus of the room and men are seated in hierarchical order from the head who sits beside the hearth. As we have seen, the household head is responsible for ensuring that the traditional laws of the *Kanun* are closely observed in every respect. Even after spending some time in northern Albania, Marjorie Senechal still felt that:

As outsiders, many aspects of daily life, especially in the mountains, would have been puzzling to us if we had not been aware of the teachings of the *kanun* . . . (It) proclaims the magnificent tradition of mountain hospitality: . . . At any time of the day or night, one must be ready to receive a guest with bread and salt and an open heart, with fire, a log of wood, and a bed. If a guest enters your house, even though he may be in blood with you, you must say to him, 'Welcome!'[15]

It is the duty of the household head to monitor those situations concerning family honour, the most important of which is hospitality. Hence a missed opportunity or the inability to offer hospitality produces shame. Nowhere is honour so much at stake as in the question of hospitality, which is considered to show the most important reflection of the family's respectful place in society. Hospitality features as a part of the very core of the *Kanun*; one of whose twelve 'Books' is devoted to honour. Post sums up the legendary nature of Albanian hospitality, and how it:

has been raised to such a high level of importance in the society that it forms an underpinning of the national consciousness. From the earliest historical observations about Albanian people, hospitality has been cited as one of their most common attributes. The nature and responsibilities of that hospitality have been recorded in stories from ancient times and codified in the *Kanun*.[16]

The concept of honour, especially in connection with hospitality, enters into every transaction and is considered of greater value than life itself. This accounts for the emphasis that Dilore placed on giving hospitality to officials whose visits were intended to force her to give up her land (see p. 76). A visitor should be greeted by the household head, and should be offered food and drink and accommodation for an indefinite period. If any harm comes to the visitor whilst in the house or on the property, the host family take full responsibility for avenging such harm. On a guest's departure, he[17] should be escorted by the household head or his family representative to the edge of his property. Harvey Sarner was impressed by the indelibility of the Albanian code of honour when interviewing members of a family who each confirmed the importance of a guest's life before their own: 'There are no foreigners in Albania, there are only guests', he was told.[18] Ismail Kadare, Albania's internationally acclaimed writer, details the intricacies of hospitality throughout his *Broken April*.

Households are known by their family name. Such is the power of honour, that the name of households held in high respect may be used in a wide area, a long way outside their property, surrounding the household in order to command respect. This serves as protection for visitors on leaving their hosts' lands. Thus I was told to mention a certain name as I travelled in the area

Figure 16. Pashke (see p. 77), having escorted the author to the village limits (the extent of her responsibility as household head). AY: Okolo, 1993

close to Bregu i Lumit; testing the validity brought remarkable respect, offers of assistance and hospitality.

Harvey Sarner gives an example of the deeply felt responsibility for guests in describing the generous hospitality offered to Jews fleeing persecution in neighbouring Serbia, Macedonia and even as far as Austria during the Second World War. He cites a case where a farmer by the name of Sulo Mecaj put his son into equal danger as his Jewish guests by hiding them all together. This was the honorable thing to do in order to give the Jews reassurance. In later years Sulo's son was asked how he felt about the situation of the added danger into which he had been put. Sarner describes his response:

The question bewildered and confused him. His reaction was that it was the proper thing to do so his father had no choice, it was a matter of honor. When asked whether he would have done as his father had done, his answer was 'of course'. Sulo's grandson, who was listening to the conversation, added his 'of course'. They both looked at me as if I had asked a foolish question, I had.[19]

A second example concerns a situation in which I myself and two others became involved when we hired a driver who thus took on the responsibility of us for the day. During a break, and away from our driver, a dispute arose in which tensions escalated to the point of violence. This dispute – details of which, it was requested 'for the honour of Albania' should not to be divulged – was fully resolved and reconciled by the man who had taken responsibility for us as his guests (our driver). He resolved the dispute which our presence had partially initiated, and ensured full reconciliation. For this to be achieved, it was necessary for all parties (about twenty people had been involved) to eat and drink together 'the meal of the blood' (the meal shared by those in reconciliation which then negates any need to take vengeance). So, in a remote wooded area, there appeared homemade cheese, bread, *raki* (strong local brandy) and bottles of beer. With a great show of sharing all with all, bottles passed back and forth and the culmination was a group photograph of all embracing one another.

Once on our way again our driver soon stopped the car. He got out and went to a tree, explaining that each time he comes to this spot he kisses the tree. He showed us the marks on the tree left by his son, who once, as a child, had been allowed to take a turn driving the truck and he had smashed into this tree. Now his father's kisses show his intense gratitude for the fact that his son was not killed.

I remarked that he would now remember the place for two events. He replied that today's was much more serious: that the death of his son would not have equalled the loss of his honour had any harm come to guests entrusted to his care!

The Guest

Thirty-eight articles define clearly how to treat 'The Guest', the first of which states 'The house of the Albanian belongs to God and the guest'.[20] A further thirteen articles make up the section on 'Violation of Hospitality', including the stipulation: 'If you do not avenge the murder of your guest, even if the murderer is a fellow-villager, you may not participate in meetings of honorable men, because you remain dishonored for the rest of your life.'[21] Further intricate instructions are given specifically on 'The Conduct of the Master of the House Toward the Guest' in fourteen articles concerning the cut of meat to be offered the guest. Even Gjeçov finds this rather excessive: 'Note: These customs seem ludicrous, but their non-observance has caused killing among people sitting at the same table.'[22] Kadare fictionalizes the situation of a case where proper hospitality had not been given:

> Gjorg walked on, looking sidelong at the ruins . . . For an instant he was still, and then, like someone who, confronted by the body of a dying man, tries to find the wound and guess what weapon has brought death near, he went to one of the corners of the house, bent down, moved a few stones, did the same thing with the other three corners, and having seen that the cornerstones had been pulled out of their beds, he knew that this was a house that had broken the laws of hospitality. Besides burning them down, there was this further treatment reserved for those houses in which the most serious crime had been committed, according to the *Kanun*: the betrayal of the guest who was under the protection of the *bessa*.[23]

All the laws are based on the evolution of the *Kanun* to suit changing times and situations; they are discussed and adapted over generations by the male members (this can of course include 'sworn virgins') of the households, chaired by the household head. This person takes responsibility for the whole of the extended family under his roof (and adjoining buildings if of the same family). As we have seen, such families contained seventy or eighty members, some were even bigger, though now fifteen to twenty is more usual, and many are smaller. Adherence to these laws has constituted the main topic of discussion amongst the men on long evenings at the hearthsides of all households through the centuries.

Amongst the households to which I was invited, I found myself one evening amidst just such a discussion. Accompanying Taulant on a visit to his great-uncle Kol we drove some miles over the winding, rutted mountain road, out of Bajram Curri, and over several ravines before stopping to leave the car at the roadside. From there we walked a few miles, mostly on muddy paths, but sometimes following invisible tracks, skirting properties and ending up in a hamlet of a few rough houses (no vehicle could reach such a spot). Taulant led my colleague and me through a cleanly brushed dirt courtyard amidst a flurry of chickens, up some steps outside a solid stone building to the first floor, and into a wooden-floored reception area. Here Kol, a man well into his seventies, greeted us. We removed our shoes and with much attention from several women we entered the house and followed Kol into the *oda* (men's room). This wooden-beamed, low-ceilinged room was freshly white-washed. The rough wooden floor was almost entirely covered by a variety of colourful handwoven wool, and goatskin floor coverings, overlapped in places by well-washed rag rugs. There was no furniture in the room other than an array of cushions with brightly coloured embroidered covers. Three small windows gave sufficient light on this summer evening without the use of the single light bulb hanging from the ceiling. On one wall hung a picture of Skanderbeg.

Kol, dressed in a worn brown suit and white 'skull cap' seated himself in his rightful place to the right of the hearthside. Other men, seated in descending age order sat on the carpeted floor, their backs to the walls. Various introductions were made, and a few questions were directed to Taulant about us. After a while Taulant asked what appeared to be burning questions of his great-uncle, to do with the practical implementation of the *Kanun*. After each query there were some moments of silence before Kol answered him with slow, carefully chosen words, pausing every couple of sentences; everyone remained silent as he spoke. Barefooted women and children gently pushed in the open doorway trying to get a better look at the unusual spectacle of foreign visitors heeding the words of their patriarch. There were a few hushing sounds from this gathering mob at the door as they each tried to quieten the others.

Taulant told his great-uncle that a family from across the valley were planning to claim the land on which a now partially destroyed derelict school stood. He asked the old man whether that family had the right to take the land. The old man remembered when the crops of another family had once been planted on that land. Other men in the room also commented, and though no arguments ensued, at times the atmosphere felt slightly fraught indicating that there was not universal agreement, but Kol ultimately had the final word.

We also learned how records are kept of boundaries without resort to written documents: male children included in negotiations, physically walk the bounds and note the placement of boulders and trees which delineate property boundaries. This ensures that when their elders have died, family representatives will still know exactly how their family lands are defined.

After a while the tension eased and women came in and served us all Turkish coffee; the men in the room talked quietly to one another, grapes were served. The serious discussion resumed on the application of the *Kanun* to different situations. Gradually the children managed to sneak a sitting space just inside the doorway. One of them was covered in scabs. As my colleague was a doctor, when discussion on the *Kanun* closed, members of the family asked him what he thought of the condition of the child. He had no difficulty in diagnosing it and was able some days later to send by relatives of relatives, a simple ointment cure. Although we were urged to stay the night, we also had obligations to other hosts, and amidst great ceremony we were escorted down the stairs and along the path between fields of high corn, to the track by which we had come.

Families 'in blood'

To be 'in blood' indicates that a family is involved in an ongoing bloodfeud. One such family whom I visited in 1995 have nine children. They live in a two-room stone house, the windows permanently closed and curtained. The oldest son, aged nineteen, had killed his neighbour (a man in his fifties). This was the culmination of a dispute over the rights of the shared irrigation stream which divides their lands one from the other. One day the neighbour's argument with the young man resulted in his hitting the nineteen-year-old. Kel, the lad, then felt this act had sufficiently offended the honour of his family to demand his taking 'blood'. The next day he went out with a knife and killed his neighbour. Kel left the area shortly after, his family claimed not to know where he was, though they clearly understood that he was still in grave danger of vengeful attack. The next two eldest children were sent away to live with relatives outside the area. The remaining six, aged three to fifteen, still live with their parents inside their home. They have not been to school for several years.

The strain on the mother of worry for her children is all too evident. In this case, unusually, the father is immune from the threat as he had grown up since childhood with the four brothers next door (and was closest in age to the one whom his son had killed). The families bent the *Kanun* rules sufficiently to ensure his immunity. He therefore (unlike his sons) is able to fetch food for the household. He is eager to negotiate reconciliation, but the neighbours insist that they are owed 'blood'.

The three boys know that they are at direct risk, the parents talk of it openly in front of them, explaining to us that the youngest (aged six) is still safe, but that it is most likely to be the eldest (aged ten) who will be the target. Although the girls are not directly at risk, they dare not venture out for fear of taunts from those around them, especially those of the feuding family. This is a form of shame which families in feud are made to feel. Many things – especially those covered by laws governing the activities of women – are considered 'shameful'. In chapter 6 we shall see how for example the failure to cover a woman's hair (with a headscarf) can be considered shameful. It is the combination of honour and shame which ensures such strict compliance with the *Kanun* laws.

Figure 17. A family who 'owes blood': the permanent death threat keeps the boys
housebound, while shame prevents any of the girls from attending
school. In this particular case, the household head (far right), has been
exempted from the threat of murder. AY: outside Bajram Curri, 1995

Mediation and Reconciliation

In the *Kanun*, there are also sections on 'Mediation' (especially in bloodfeuds)
and 'The Guarantee'. In outlining reconciliation between the family of the
victim and the family of the murderer, there is further instruction on the
accomplishment of this reconciliation and the part of guarantors which
requires a mediator between the two families. Although it is stipulated that
a mediator 'may be a man or a woman, a boy or a girl, or even a priest',[24]
the role of the mediator is usually taken on by the revered (male) elders of
the tribes and villages. This should also be a role for 'sworn virgins', though
none mentioned to me their having taken part in a mediation.

A successful mediation may be achieved by agreement of a financial
payment or the sharing of a piece of land. Once reconciliation is achieved, in
the case of a bloodfeud, there is a celebration with the 'The Meal of Blood',
as mentioned above. Those who attend this ritual meal are the mediators,
the victim and his relatives and friends who all go to the house of the murderer
to share a meal together provided by the murderer's family.[25]

The anthropologist Carleton Coon spent time in northern Albania in the 1920s primarily studying the physical features of men and women.[26] His detailed report also comments on the extraordinarily high percentage of violent deaths in the male population.[27] Besides this elimination of young men through violent means, there has more recently also been migration in search of work elsewhere, in Tirana or even abroad accounting for an increasing shortage of men in the highlands.[28]

In summary, interpretations of the laws of the *Kanun* form the basis of northern Albanian morality and govern rules of behaviour on every level. The *besa* or oath of an Albanian is understood to be an honourable lifelong commitment: 'sworn virgins' also feel this commitment to their oath whether or not it is formally made. This honour is most strongly associated with the rules governing hospitality and the way guests must be treated. Kazuhiko Yamamoto has researched this topic thoroughly and suggests that the guest takes on a god-like status, connected with an ancient pagan 'cult of ancestors', and must be treated as such to prevent retribution.[29] Families 'in blood' whose honour is tainted, live in alternating fear or shame until the conflict is resolved.

Taking into account the very patriarchal nature of traditional Albanian society and its ongoing necessity for male household heads, all these factors contribute to the continuing tradition of another kind of 'man' to keep the oath of the 'sworn virgin'.

Notes

1. Gjeçov, S. (1989), *Kanuni i Lekë Dukagjinit* (The Code of Lek Dukagjini), translated by L. Fox, New York: Gjonlekaj Publishing Co. p. 130.

2. Gjeçov (1989), *Kanuni i Lekë Dukagjinit*. In this, Dukagjini differed from Skanderbeg who did not consider all men equal.

3. Gjeçov (1989), *Kanuni i Lekë Dukagjinit*, Article 598, p. 130.

4. Gjeçov, S. (1989), *Kanuni i Lekë Dukagjinit*. Article 270, p. 82 states, 'The common good is placed before private damage', and Article 360, p. 92 states, 'The common good overrides special interests'.

5. Gjeçov (1989), *Kanuni i Lekë Dukagjinit*, p. 216.

6. The *Kanun* of Skanderbeg was confined to a rather limited area, whereas the *Kanun* of Lekë Dukagjini was followed throughout the northern mountains, in Dukagjin, Shkodër, Western Kosov@ and even amongst the Albanian populations elsewhere in parts of Serbia, Montenegro and Macedonia (see Gjeçov (1989), *Kanuni i Lekë Dukagjinit*, p. xvii).

7. Illia, I.F. (1993), *Kanuni i Skanderbegut* (The Code of Skanderbeg), Shkodër: Botim i Argjipeshkvisë së Shkodërs, Article 984, p. 74.

8. Illia (1993), *Kanuni i Skanderbegut*, Article 985, p. 75.

9. Illia (1993), *Kanuni i Skanderbegut*, Article 989 pp. 74–5. Note that it is not the girl who is being considered in connection with possible shame caused by change of heart, but the family.

10. Backer, B. (1979), *Behind the Stone Walls: Changing 'Household Organization among the Albanians of Kosovo*, Oslo: PRIO-publication S-8/79, p. 154.

11. This was one of the nun-type 'virgins'. At the time of the death of the priest to whom she had acted as a holy servant, she was forty years old. However she 'shocked the country-side by eloping with a Gusinje Moslem. No one dared follow to take vengeance in such a dangerous district, but it was piously hoped that she would pay the price of her crime in hell'; Durham, M.E. (1928), *Some Tribal Origins, Laws and Customs of the Balkans*, London: Allen & Unwin, p. 195.

12. Whitaker (1981), 'A Sack for Carrying Things', p. 151.

13. Gordon, J. and C.J. (1927), *Two Vagabonds in Albania*, New York: Dodd, Mead; London: John Lane, The Bodley Head, pp. 238–9.

14. However, he makes no mention of the absence of women from that room. Pichler, R. (11 June 1999), 'History and Tradition: Producing Myths of the 'Pure' National Character', conference paper 'Myths in the Politics of Transition', Albanian Studies, University of London, p. 9.

15. Quoting the *Kanun*, Senechal, M. (1997), *Long Life to Your Children! A Portrait of High Albania*, Amherst: University of Massachusetts Press, p. 33.

16. Post (1998), *Women in Modern Albania*, Jefferson, North Carolina; London: McFarland, p. 32.

17. Only 'he' is mentioned here, since women are not traditionally accorded the same honour (foreign women have been treated as honorary men).

18. Sarner, H. (1997), *Rescue in Albania: One Hundred Percent of Jews in Albania Rescued from Holocaust*, Cathedral City, California: Brunswick Press; Boston, Massachusetts: The Frosina Foundation, p. 63.

19. Sarner (1997), *Rescue in Albania*, p. 50.

20. Gjeçov (1989), *Kanuni i Lekë Dukagjinit*, Article 602, p. 132.

21. Gjeçov (1989), *Kanuni i Lekë Dukagjinit*, Article 651, section c, p. 136.

22. Gjeçov (1989), *Kanuni i Lekë Dukagjinit*, addition to Article 659, p. 138.

23. Kadare, I. (1991), *Broken April*, London: Harvill, Harper Collins, pp. 41–2.

24. Gjeçov (1989), *Kanuni i Lekë Dukagjinit*, Article 669, p. 138.

25. Gjeçov (1989), *Kanuni i Lekë Dukagjinit*, Article CXXXVIII, p. 184.

26. Coon, C. (1970), *The Mountain of Giants: a Racial and Cultural Study of the North Albanian Mountain Ghegs*, Cambridge, Massachusetts: Harvard University. Papers of the Peabody Museum, (1950), vol. 23, no. 3.

27. Albanologist Philip Wynn draws attention to Coon's theories concerning the rationalization of these ritualized killings, in a barren mountainous area where human society is living on the edge of mere survival: 'There is only one universal immemorial method of disposing of excess population under these circumstances. That is the method found in the Rif, in the Caucasus, in the Kafir country of Afghanistan, and in many other places – feuding. If enough males are killed off, the population remains constant'; (1950) *The Mountains of Giants*, p. 27.

28. Far fewer women than men migrate in search of work, though some have been abducted and sold into prostitution in Italy and Greece.

29. Yamamoto, K. (1998), 'The Origin of Ethics and Social Order in a Society Without State Power', Conference paper, Fourth International Congress on Physicological Anthropology, Zagreb, vol. 5, no. 365, p. 7, *Collegium Anthropologicum*. Further comment on Yamamoto's theories will be made in Chapter 4.

4

Who are the 'Sworn Virgins'?

Because it is such a powerful force in the world today, the Western Judeo-Christian tradition is often accepted as the arbiter of 'natural' behavior of humans. If Europeans and their descendant nations of North America accept something as normal, then anything different is seen as abnormal. Such a view ignores the great diversity of human existence.

W.L. Williams, *The Spirit of the Flesh: Sexual Diversity in American Indian Culture*[1]

Origins

No documentation has yet been discovered to explain the origin of the phenomenon of the 'sworn virgins'; nor has any date of origin been agreed upon, though several researchers have referred to the Amazon legends of Ancient Greece.[2] Tatomir Vukanović made an ethnographic study specifically of 'sworn virgins' amongst the southern Slavs during the periods 1935–48 and 1952–60, and gives many references to the findings of earlier writers on 'sworn virgins', including some as far afield as Turkey. He mentions two gypsy 'sworn virgins' from Kosov@, one of whom he met in 1958.[3] Other writers on the subject during the nineteenth and early twentieth century mentioned 'sworn virgins' in the course of their wider studies of Albanian society. Vukanović's article outlines the theory that the phenomenon originates from the survival of a genetic link to the legendary Amazon warrior-women of a lost matriarchal age in ancient Greece. He proposes that this could even have been a worldwide phenomenon.[4] Albanian scholar, E. Chabsi called the 'sworn virgins', 'Amazons',[5] a connection which has also been made by Milenko Filipović, Andromaqi Gjergji, Karl Kaser and others.[6] Mariana Gusić attributes the origin of 'sworn virgins' with the 'cult of Virgo' and was the first to relate it to the custom of idolatry or the veneration of relics.[7] However, Mirko Bajraktarović disputes this, citing the improbability of the propagation of the cult by the minimal numbers of churchgoers living in the agrarian era.[8] He explains the continued existence of the phenomenon by the force which guards or protects a house – the guardianship and preservation of the 'cult of ancestors' and the 'cult of house and earth'. Yamamoto makes the case that the perpetuation of the *Kanun* itself is based on the strength of belief in a 'pagan religion whose main features are animism and ancestor worship'.[9] It seems likely that the birth of the phenomenon has its roots in this earlier pre-Christian tradition. In attempting to trace the origins of the phonemenon, Gusić stresses the need 'to search for a dualist paleological link between the earth and the sea cult of Virgo ('the virginal one').[10]

During the past 150 years, many foreign geographers, travellers, anthropologists, and historians have commented on meeting occasional 'sworn virgins', but only a few have made any detailed study of them. No documentation has been found of their existence before the nineteenth century. However, since mention of them is made in the *Kanun*, dating from at least the fifteenth century, this would suggest that 'sworn virgins' were already a part of traditional life, orally recorded over the centuries.

Research under Communism

Bajraktarović published the results of his research on material gathered from interviews with several 'sworn virgins' during the first half of the twentieth century. Two of them were brought up as boys from birth. One became a man by her parents' choice as a teenager, two chose this option rather than go through with a specific arranged marriage and a further three made their own choices (the author does not detail why).[11]

Branimir Bratanić founded a project producing a series of books of ethnographical 'Questions.'[12] He systematically organized for this set of 152 groups of questions to be sent to all parts of Yugoslavia with the intention of completing an ethnographic map of the country, showing the places and numbers of all kinds of artifacts and ethnographic phenomena. 'Sworn virgins' were included in the subjects for research.[13]

Research work written by Westerners (mostly published since the 1960s) on the subject of 'sworn virgins', particularly relating to Albania, was based on data collected before 1940, and most assumed that the tradition had died out.[14]

However, during the 1980s René Grémaux visited Durgjane Gllavolla, a 'sworn virgin' in Kosov@, and interviewed relatives and acquaintances of three others, some in Montenegro. He wrote three articles resulting from his research. Grémaux reported in detail on four 'sworn virgins', two of whom were still living at the time of his writing. He also provided analysis of these cases, some of which will be referred to elsewhere in this book.[15]

Changing Gender in Albania

In Western society it is becoming increasingly accepted that people who perceive themselves as belonging to the opposite sex from their physiological bodies and identify themselves as such should not be regarded as dysfunctional, but rather should be assisted both physically and emotionally, in transforming themselves into the sex of their choice. To this end the use of hormones, operations and psychological counselling over a period of sometimes several years is available in more affluent societies.[16] As will be seen in chapter 7, changes are more often made from male to female than *vice versa*.[17]

In traditional Albanian society there is no such sophisticated (and expensive) surgical assistance for social and psychological transition. However, the reasons for the female-to-male cross gender role taken on by the women I have interviewed in Albania (and also those in the surrounding regions), have less to do with the individual than the social, economic and cultural situation into which they are born. Early records refer predominantly to this as the only acceptable alternative to not marrying the man to whom a woman was betrothed. Another strong reason to encourage the change of gender is in order to be eligible to become a family head and a legal heir – an essential role to be filled in every household. Lack of a son of sufficient age and integrity (representing honour for a family) may bring shame. Such was the case reported by Samardžić of Stana who specifically comments that the 'shame' brought to her family of five daughters and no sons, was the reason for her change of gender.[18] Peristiany discusses honour and shame as 'two poles of an evaluation'.[19] In Albania, it is the importance of upholding honour which frequently leads to a bloodfeud.[20] In order to cross the boundary from a woman's world to a male domain, it is necessary to change sex socially: this is done by dressing as a man and socially engaging in activities limited to men.

The Question of Homosexuality

It may be felt that there is some ambiguity when it comes to the sexuality of these 'sworn virgins.' Quite apart from its being hard to initiate discussion of what is considered a very intimate topic, there is the added fact that their vow of celibacy makes it difficult, and in many cases inappropriate to pry too far into the private lives of these women.

It is even hard to get a clear sense of any kind of underlying sexuality amongst the 'sworn virgins' due to the unspoken and taboo nature of the subject of sex in rural Albanian society. As Tom Parfitt writes:

You swallow hard before you mention sex in this ultraconservative area. It is completely taboo. 'Why should I miss having sex when my family is already so large?' says Lule. 'Work is the most important thing in my life.' Like the other avowed virgins she looks utterly uncomprehending when asked about lesbianism; she had difficulty in comprehending the concept of female homosexuality. Procreation is the only reason for sex, and then only within wedlock.[21]

It has been suggested that some might feign incomprehension as a defence mechanism to avoid dealing with this taboo subject. An added complication in the field was having to conduct my interviews through an interpreter who could feel implicated in the potentially dangerous or incriminating situation had one of the 'sworn virgins' admitted to any kind of sexual activity. Taking the suggestion further, since both the 'sworn virgin' and the interpreter would know that breaking of the oath of celibacy could damage her reputation in her own community and further, it would then follow that both parties would be implicated in bringing dishonour to Albania in the eyes of a foreigner. As such, a 'sworn virgin' would be more likely in any case to remain silent on this topic. However, my own interpretation is that the concept of lesbianism itself is an alien one to all the 'sworn virgins' I met, and even to some interpreters. It is certainly my understanding that the actual occurrence of a sexual relationship between a 'sworn virgin' and another person – given both the vow, and the proximity of others in their lives – is rare, and probably non-existent. Furthermore as part of their masculinized attitudes, 'sworn virgins' would feel dishonoured by speaking about their feelings and emotions; it would damage their reputations as honourable men. Whitaker drew information from Johannes von Hahn to conclude that:

There was a permissive attitude to male homosexuality, particularly when shepherds were away from feminine company in the hills. In these situations homosexual attachments were common and were seen as the expected behaviour, particularly of younger men . . . At the same time however, the idea that womenfolk back in the valleys might wish to indulge in lesbian associations was viewed partly with abhorrence, and partly with a disbelief that any pleasure could be associated with such activities.[22]

The fact that female homosexuality was not mentioned in the law in Albania banning homosexuality between men which was only amended in 1995, adds credibility to the theory that the concept of female homosexuality had not even been considered.

Although Grémaux found female homosexuality highly unusual, he however claimed to have heard of occasional cases. In his account of these cases it comes across clearly that because of the sexual aspect of their situation, they were not fully accepted as 'sworn virgins' within their own communities. Grémaux noted what he interpreted as sexual tendencies towards females in the cases of Mikas and Stana, 'albeit in a rather limited and repressed way'. For example, Stana revealed that although she and others knew that she had taken an oath not to marry, had she not, she would have married a woman. But once again, it is difficult to avoid our own cultural interpretations of this response. It could be inferred, from this statement that Stana's choice to become a 'sworn virgin' may have been driven by latent lesbian inclinations, it could equally be inferred, however, that Stana feels the need to strengthen her case for being treated and respected as a male by making the same sexual innuendos or remarks about women as a man in that society would. This interpretation would certainly be supported by Stana's parting words to her interviewer: 'Stana asked whether I would sincerely tell her whether in my heart I consider her a male.'[23] This indicates that the desire to have absolute status as a man may supersede sexual inclination as a motivating factor in her remarks. Grémaux continues:

> Although I found absolutely no trace of liaisons with women, cohabitation of masculine sworn virgins with female partners is not completely unknown. I know of three such couples in two of which a sexual relationship is actually indicated. At least two of these three couples were bound by 'blood-sisterhood', a kind of ritual or spiritual kinship that, however does not usually include living together.[23]

Of the third couple he comments that they were only mentioned 'briefly in a book' and that the author's words 'leave us guessing at the nature of this relationship, and no other known source provides information about it'.[24]

According to Vukanović, 'sworn virgins' were in some places ill reputed for 'certain abnormal sexual relations' with their blood-sisters.[25]

The notion of lesbianism amongst 'virgins' who have sworn the oath is therefore a taboo and possibly an alien concept, where access to credible accounts and any discussion is extremely limited. There does appear to be a kind of mystification of the status of these women as concerns their sexuality, and there is a tendency for some authors on the topic to regard these women as lesbians. Whilst instances of such relationships cannot be altogether ruled out, we need to be aware of the kind of mythologization of these stories as they get passed down from ancestor to ancestor, village to village and beyond. It is necessary to be aware of this 'Chinese whispers' effect, in conducting our research and possibly even to question the absolute credibility of sources quoting 'a story that was told by a villager' and even of authors who cite examples from other authors who themselves never actually met the 'sworn virgins' in question. We need to be concerned with authenticity in our reporting of sources which question the sexual practise of these women who have sworn to lifelong celibacy in a society where pride and honour is of importance above all else.

Three Kinds of 'Sworn Virgin'

'Sworn virgins' may be identified according to three types: firstly those whose choice was made in childhood, at or even before birth by parents; secondly those whose choice came after puberty. A third variation of 'sworn virgin', believed no longer to be in existence, is the semi-religious one.

'Sworn virgins' of the first category, *vajze e betuar* ('sworn girl': *betuar* comes from the same linguistic root as *besa*), seem to be the most common today. For example Shkurtan's (pp. 78–9) parents gave her the role when the death of her older brother, during Shkurtan's childhood, brought this new need to the family. According to the rules of the *vajze e betuar*, a daughter will be brought up in preparation to become the household head. In this role she will be permitted eventually to inherit the home and property which, according to customary law is not permissable in any other circumstance for a woman. The term used in the case of Stefan in the award-winning Yugoslav film *Virdžina* is *mashkull* (male).[26] The youngest 'sworn virgin' of all those whom I interviewed in Albania (see Medi, pp. 85–87), as in the film, was the youngest in a family with only daughters, born to poor and elderly parents. The immediate seen need for a son in the near future to take the lead in the family and to inherit the family's meagre home, spurred them to announce the birth of a son, and to bring up this third daughter as such. In both situations their fathers were their models with whom they spent much of their time during their childhood and adolescence.

I have found no distinction in the term used for those brought up as boys from our second category and those who make the change later in life. From most earlier sources it seems that the usual reason for a woman to make the life-changing decision for herself, was in order to avoid an undesirable marriage without bringing dishonour to her and her fiancé's family. In the case of Raba (see p. 82), this concern with honour was felt even towards a dead fiancé's family. This releases the fiancé from the tie, and he may choose to marry another; an option not open to the 'sworn virgin' whose subsequent marriage to anyone could set a bloodfeud in motion by so dishonouring the fiancé even if he did marry someone else.

Whitaker indicates that Durham also found that refusal to marry a specific man was the most usual precursor to a woman becoming a 'sworn virgin', but that in this category, they did not assume male dress.[27] Whitaker suggests an additional reason which could inspire a woman to take the oath: 'when all of her brothers have been killed, she might herself assume the masculine role, abjure all thought of marriage, and take on the duty of exacting revenge for her dead sibling'. In such a situation she would already have sufficient cause to become a man in order to inherit the home and head the family when her parents died. Such was the case of the guide of travel writer Bernard Newman with whom he travelled for days before finding out that he was in fact a woman (see plate 2 and text p. 7). Her last surviving brother had been killed a few weeks before her scheduled wedding day.[28] In all cases the gender change is made in order to preserve family honour.

My own findings did not show that the avoidance of marriage to a specific partner was the reason for choosing to become a 'sworn virgin'. The most usual response I was given was the immediate or forseen future need for a household head and inheritor of the home.

Bajraktarović cites the nineteenth-century Austrian diplomat and Alban-ologist Johannes Georg von Hahn concerning a tendency of young women to marry undesirable husbands (or taking the oath to become a 'sworn virgin'). He notes that this was higher amongst those who were less willing to hand over all the family property to the church (according to law as it operated in the time and area of his research) if she were unwilling to marry her betrothed. He also claims that a 'sworn virgin' could even be allowed to marry later if the reasons for which she had taken the vows, later disappeared.[29] This, however, seems unlikely in light of the fact that widows rarely remarried (where levirate was practised they automatically became the wife of their brother-in-law), and even a young girl might never marry, if her betrothed died before the wedding date (as in the case of Raba, p. 82).

The third type of 'sworn virgin' is more of an anomaly and fits less well into the family structure. *Murgéshë* or *morga* (nun) were thought to have been fairly common in the period 1715–1912, and by 1907, Grémaux notes that 'according to Schulz, the predominantly Catholic tribes of Malesi in northern Albania counted about 200 such "virgins".'[30] The *murgéshë* 'virgins' can be compared to the female *sadhins* of India (see p. 112) in that they were celibate and normally donned male attire. They wore black and behaved as nuns, sometimes as assistants to priests, but living at home. There are brief mentions of such people in several accounts of life in northern Albania. Grémaux made a study from earlier sources of these 'virgins' and their connections with the influential Catholic Church in northern Albania. He found evidence of one instance of 'the consecration of manlike virgins' in the work of von Hahn.[31] Grémaux concludes:

Notwithstanding growing Franciscan aloofness towards the worldly Albanian 'virgins', however, they continued to be easily associated with one another. Whether the friars liked it or not, these 'virgins' were to a certain degree their natural allies, inasmuch as both groups were committed to celibacy. Friars and 'virgins' were outsiders in a society obsessed by marriage and procreation. According to the standards of that society, the friar was not a genuine man, nor the 'virgin' a real woman. The fact that the friars were unarmed and wore robes whereas the 'virgins could wear trousers and carry arms' highlights the marginal position they shared in this tribal society.[32]

He draws this information also in part from the findings of Edith Durham and Carleton Coon. 'Sworn virgins' of this type whom Durham actually met wore women's dress and usually became servants to one of the priests of the Third Order of St Francis.[33] Stahl comments that in 1910 the leaders of the Christian community 'came up with a law according to which it was henceforth forbidden for girls to declare themselves nuns, except for those who enter a convent'.[34]

Despite the use by writers of various terms for 'sworn virgins', I never met one who applied any of the terms to themselves, preferring their self-perceptions simply to be prestigious men.[35] However, most would not deny their transition from having been female. Some expected to be spoken of and addressed as men, and would be very offended if addressed otherwise (Shkurtan is one of these), others were quite at ease being grammatically treated as female. In Albanian, as in most European languages other than English, it is hard to speak of a person, or even to them without adjusting verbs and adjectives to fit the gender of the person to whom or about whom a conversation is addressed. Several of the 'sworn virgins' I met had already masculinized their names, or had grown up with masculine names.

A familiar term, one used commonly amongst Albanians in the north to discuss 'sworn virgins', though not to or between the 'virgins' themselves, is the term *burrneshë*. The meaning of this word is exemplified in the greeting which Post noticed between women, also in the northern part of Albania: '*a je burrneshë?*' The word *burrneshë* is a feminine word, and the phrase means literally 'are you a man-woman', but is understood as 'are you as strong as a man?'[36] This can be seen in contrast to the more common greeting '*a je lodh?*' (are you tired?).

Some Exceptions

Bajraktarović cites the unusual case of a 'sworn virgin' from a village of Hishora, near Prizren in Kosov@ who was given the male name Dilyosh and was brought up as a son. Eventually he went to fight in the Second World War in Trieste and was wounded. On discovery, in hospital, that Dilyosh was a woman, she was immediately demobilized. According to Bajraktarović, when it became locally known in 1951 that Dilyosh was not a man, she married and later bore two children. Her mother was most distressed that her 'only son' had married and changed her name to Fatima. This unusual case was also written up later by Grémaux.[37]

Barbara Demick reports on another exceptional case, that of Sugare Xhaferaj, a 'sworn virgin' who lives in the village of Uji i Shenjte (Sacred Water) on the Kir River. She was aged seventy-eight at the time of their meeting in 1996. Sugare was widowed at the age of twenty-eight, and was pregnant with her fourth child at the time. She had no brothers and her sons were very young. To retain the property and work the land, she started to wear men's clothing and also to show that she was not available for marriage. From that time on other men addressed her as a man, and her children called her 'father'. At the age of seventy-four Sugare resumed wearing women's clothing.[38]

Film and Fiction

'Sworn virgins' have been used as a subject of fiction, film and theatre. The film *Virdžina* has been discussed elsewhere (p. 58). Set in nineteenth-century Montenegro, the opening shots show the deep distress of the peasant parents at the birth of yet another girl. The father at first threatens to kill the newborn, then resolves to announce it as a boy. There is widespread rejoicing throughout the village and surrounding areas and (Orthodox) church bells ring out the good news of the birth of a son (Stefan), whereas only commiseration had been offered at the birth of each of the father's daughters. As Stefan grows up, Karanavić portrays the emotional strains which might be expected concerning the sexual identity of a pubescent girl forced into a male role from birth. Stefan's breasts are stunted from growth by the pressure of tight bandages wound around her upper body. The film shows Stefan's growth into puberty and that the onset of menstruation did not interfere with her social role as a developing man. The family is presented with a dilemma when eventually Stefan's mother (who dies in childbirth) bears a son. At this point it is Stefan who takes the decision to give the newborn to another family, whose household head is a well-disguised 'sworn virgin'; thus Stefan's own status, on the death of her father, is confirmed as a household head.

Nita is a four-act tragedy by Josip Rela (1895–1966), a native of Zadar in Croatia, of Albanian descent. It concerns a young woman abducted by a

Turkish soldier. Her saviour, Zef, first kills the soldier and then is obliged to flee to escape vengeance from the Turks. Nita vows to wait for his return, but as time passes and marriage to another is planned by her family, she takes the only honourable option and swears eternal virginity in front of the priest and the council of village elders. Shortly after this, Zef returns; as Nita cannot go back on her word she sees suicide as the only solution to the tragic situation.[39]

The children's book *Pran of Albania* by Elizabeth Cleveland Miller, tells the story of a young girl growing up in northern Albania early in the nineteenth century in traditional rural society. Pran's mother tells her daughter, with great sadness, that Pran's betrothal has been arranged. The daughter had her own secret wishes but knows they may not be voiced; she learns that she has an honourable option to marrying the one not of her choice, and declares that she will 'take the vow'. The happy ending to the story defies tradition: it turns out that the man to whom she is betrothed is in fact the very same young man whom she had once met momentarily and for whom she had vowed to marry no other. The vow is abandoned and we can suppose that the couple lived happily ever after.[40] In real life it is unlikely that a *besa* would so easily be set aside.

Recently widespread attention to 'sworn virgins' has been drawn by the writer Alice Munro. The theme of Munro's story, *The Albanian Virgin*, as its title suggests, is loosely based on the 'sworn virgin' tradition. The fictional account set early in the twentieth century, tells of Charlotte, a young American woman accompanying older friends on an Adriatic cruise. In Montenegro, she escapes the boredom of her companions by taking a local guide and horses to explore inland. It turns out that the guide takes her through land where he is in feud and he is shot and killed. (In real life, being accompanied by a woman, especially a foreigner, should have saved him from this killing). The heroine's horse falls and she is seriously injured. Saved, taken into the Albanian mountains and eventually completely revived, Lottar (as Charlotte became named) finds she is immersed in Albanian peasant and family life (from which she seems to make surprisingly little effort to escape). After more than a year, she learns the cost of her living when she is dressed in wedding finery and is about to be sold off in marriage to a Muslim from another village. However, Lottar who has already met a 'sworn virgin', is saved from this marriage by the local Franciscan priest who had helped her recovery: he arrives in anger and saves her by speedily arranging for the necessary witnesses before whom she can swear lifelong celibacy and become a 'virgin'. The priest later helps her, now living as a man, to return to the outside world, in fear that (although a 'virgin') she will still be sold in marriage to a Muslim. However, this motive ignores the traditional strength of acceptance of the *besa* of virginity which should have saved her from any further suggestions of marriage even though she was a foreigner.[41]

'Sworn Virgins' Today

There are even now, still a number of such women living as men in northern Albania and the surrounding areas. They are not always recognizable, for once their parents, or they themselves (usually as children or adolescents), make the vow to become male, they dress and behave accordingly – and as such are totally acccepted and even revered within their communities. By the same token, it may well be that several more known to have been women are still living as men. Few in Albania are aware of the phenomenon, and fewer still consider it of any interest. People living in the rural areas of northern Albania, who know of the tradition, consider it so much a part of normal life that it does not stand out as anything exceptional. This was confirmed for me when a friend suddenly became aware of three individuals of his acquaintance, living in different parts of Shkodër whom, on some reflection, he realized were indeed 'sworn virgins' (these are the three Shkodrans whose stories are told on pp. 87–8). To quote another informant: '"Sworn virgins" are not a phenomenon, they are just a fact of life; the way they act is the way they organize their lives.'[42]

In the following chapter we shall consider the lives of individual 'sworn virgins' and find out how they have each adapted to the role which society provides them with. It will become clear that none fits exactly into the prototype, but that each has found the niche which meets the needs of her immediate family.

Notes

1. Williams, W.L. (1988), *The Spirit and the Flesh: Sexual Diversity in American Indian Culture*, Boston: Beacon Press, p. 1.

2. See Vukanović, T. (1961), 'Virdžine' (virgins), *Glasnik Muzeja Kosova i Metohije*, VI, Prishtina p. 112; and Bajraktarović M. (1965–6), 'The Problem of *Tobelije*', *Glasnik Ethnografskog Museja*, Belgrade: Knjiga 28–29, pp. 273–86.

3. Vukanović (1961), 'Virdžine', pp. 97–8.

4. Vukanović (1961), 'Virdžine', pp. 79–112.

5. Quoted in Bajraktarović (1965–6), 'The Problem of *Tobelije*,' p. 131.

6. Filipović, M. (1982) discusses 'Women as Heads of Villages and Groups among the South Slavs and Certain Other Balkan Peoples' from the fifteenth century, see Hammel, E.A. et al., (eds), *Among the People: Native Yugoslav Ethnography: Selected*

Writings of Milenko S. Filipović, Ann Arbor, Michigan: Papers in Slavic Philology no. 3, Department of Slavic Languages and Literature, University of Michigan; Gjergji, A. (1963), 'Gjurmë të Matriarktit në disa Doke të Dikurshme të Jetës Familjare' (Traces of Matriarchy in some Former Customs of Family Life), *Buletini i Universitetit të Tiranës* (Shkencat Shoqërore) pp, 284–92; and Kaser, K. (1994), 'Die Mannfrau in den Patriarchalen Gesellschaften des Balkans und der Mythos vom Matriarchat' (Woman as Honorary Man in the Patriarchal Societies of the Balkans and the Myth of Matriarchy), *L'Homme Zeitschrift für Feministische Geschichtswissenschaft*, vol. 5, no. 1.

7. Gusić, M. in Bajraktarović (1965–6), 'The Problem of *Tobelije*', p. 131.

8. Bajraktarović (1965–6), 'The Problem of *Tobelije*', p. 131.

9. Yamamoto, K. (1999), 'The Origin of Ethics in a Society Without State Power', Conference paper, Fourth International Congress on Physiological Anthropology, Zagreb, *Collegium Anthropologicum*, vol. 23, no. 1, p. 1.

10. In Bajraktarović (1965–6), 'The Problem of *Tobelije*', p. 131.

11. Bajraktarović (1965–6), 'The Problem of *Tobelije*,' pp. 273–86.

12. Bratanić, B. (1966), *Upitnica Etnološkog Atlas*, (Atlas of Ethnological Questions), Zagreb: Filozofski Fakultet u Zagrebu.

13. Unfortunately, not only did Bratanić die before the work was completed but with the break-up of Yugoslavia, the series was discontinued.

14. For example, Berit Backer did not meet any 'sworn virgins', though she reported that there were some in neighbouring villages to Isniq, (Kosov@) where she did her fieldwork. She also commented that there is no complementary role found among men: (1979), *Behind the Stone Walls*, p. 308; Dickemann, M. refers to 'fragmentary' modern art (1997), 'The Balkan Sworn Virgin: a Traditional European Transperson' in Bullough V. and V. and Elias, J. (eds) *Gender Blending*, Amherst, New York: Prometheus, p. 248; Coon uses the material he collected over two decades earlier, he mentions meeting two 'sworn virgins' (1950), *The Mountains of Giants*; Kaser (1994), 'Die Mannfrau in den Patriarchalen Gesellschaften des Balkans und der Mythos vom Matriarchat'; Shryock, A.J. (Jan. 1988), 'Autonomy, Entanglement, and the Feud: Prestige Structures and Gender Values in Highland Albania', *Anthropological Quarterly*, vol. 61, no. 1, pp. 113–18; Stahl, P.H. (1986), 'The Albanians' (ch. III) in *Household Village and Village Confederation in Southeastern Europe*, Boulder, Colorado: East European Monographs (no. 200), pp. 110–11; Whitaker, I. (1981), 'A Sack for Carrying Things: the Traditional Role of Women in Northern Albanian Society' in *Anthropological Quarterly*, vol. 54, p. 151.

15. Grémaux, R. (1989), 'Mannish Women of the Balkan Mountains' in Bremmer, J. (ed.), *From Sappho to de Sade: Moments in the History of Sexuality, New York; London: Routledge*, pp. 143–71 and (1994), 'Woman Becomes Man in the Balkans' in Herdt, G. (ed.), *Third Sex, Third Gender: Beyond Sexual Dimorphism in Culture and History*, New York: Zone Books, pp. 241–81.

The life history of Stana Cerović, one of the 'sworn virgins' whom Grémaux attempted to visit was written up by Medihan Samardžić and published in Banja Luka: Samardžić, M. (19–20 Jan. 1991), 'Muško sam, jado jadna' (I am Male: on the Trail of Old Customs: Sworn Virgin), *Glas*, pp. 13–14.

16. In Britain this has been provided on occasion by the National Health Service where the need is proved justified.

17. See Dea Birkett's discussion in her (5 Aug. 1999), 'Mutilation Won't Make a Man a Woman', *The Guardian*, G2, p. 5.

18. Samardžić, (19–20 Jan. 1991), pp. 13–14.

19. Peristiany, J.G. (ed.) (1965), *Honour and Shame: The Values of Mediterranean Society*, London: Wiedenfeld & Nicolson, p. 9.

20. See Appendix 2.

21. Parfitt, T. (1 June 1997), 'Land Beyond Time', *Spectrum*, p. 2.

22. Von Hahn wrote in the first half of the nineteenth century; Whitaker, I. (1981), 'A Sack for Carrying Things: the Traditional Role of Women in Northern Albanian Society,' *Anthropological Quarterly*, vol. 54, p. 150.

23. Samardžić (19–20 Jan. 1991), 'Muško sam, jado jadna!', p. 14.

24. Grémaux (1994), 'Woman Becomes Man in the Balkans,' p. 272.

25. Quoted by Grémaux (1994), 'Woman Becomes Man in the Balkans,' p. 271.

26. Karanović, S. (1991), *Virdžina*. This was the last official film to be made as a co-production between Croatian, Serbian and French companies. The story was based on one read by Director in a newspaper, concerning a woman in 1944. Karanović believed this to be the last existing case.

27. Whitaker, I. (1968), 'Tribal Structure and National Politics in Albania, 1910–1950' in Lewis, I.M. (ed.), *History and Social Anthropology*, London; New York: Tavistock Publications, footnote 14, p. 285.

28. Newman, B. (1936), *Albanian Backdoor*, London: Jenkins, pp. 260–1.

29. Bajraktarović (1965–6), 'The Problem of the *Tobelije*', p. 131. In the case of Dilore (see p. 76), she merely became the older brother to her new half-brother.

30. Grémaux (1992), 'Franciscan Friars,' p. 374, quotes Schulz, E. (5 Oct. 1907), 'Albanisches Mannwiebertum' (Albanian Mannish Women), *Die Woche*, p. 1763.

31. Grémaux (1992), 'Franciscan Friars, pp. 364–5.

32. Grémaux (1992), 'Franciscan Friars', p. 372.

33. Durham, M.E. (1928), *Some Tribal Origins, Laws and Customs of the Balkans*, London: Allen & Unwin, p. 195.

34. Stahl (1986), 'The Albanians', p. 112.

35. Anthropologists have used various terms either in Albanian or their own languages for 'sworn virgins.' Shryock termed them *virghereshe* (a Tosk word meaning 'committed to virginity'). Other writers gave various similar names to the marriage refuser: Edith Durham – 'Albanian virgin', Andromaqi Gjergji – *virgjin*, Ernesto Cozzi's *virgjereshe* and René Grémaux's *vergjinéshë*, all probably from the Italian root of the same word. Grémaux also uses 'sworn virgin' as do contemporary anthropologists, or the alternative 'avowed virgin.'

In Serbian, several terms have been used: *muškobani* or *muškobanja*, *muškobara*, *muškaraca*, *muškara*, *maškadanka*, *muškudan*, *mužana*, *muš* (all based on the word for 'man'), *ostajnica* and *ostanata devojka* (she who stays [at home]). Others are *baba devojka*, *žena devojka* and *stara cura* (all meaning 'old maid'), *starosedelki* (one who remains unmarried), *usedjelica*, *usidjelica*, *posedjelica*, *posidjelica* (these last four meaning 'spinster'), and *prizetresa*. Some terms found in Montenegro are *virdžineša, vidjneš, baša, harambaša, tombelija.* Similarly the term *tobelija* in Bosnia and *tybeli* in Kosov@ (bound by a vow, which Barjaktarović claims originates from the Turkish word *tobyé*, meaning 'a vow') describe the situation, also *adumica, Ragibaga.* In Macedonia the term *Prekar maškudanka* has been used. In Croatian the phrase *zavjetovana djevojka* is used whereas, Paul Stahl found the Turkish form *sadik* for Muslim 'sworn virgins' (meaning 'honest' or 'just'). In Istria the word *sam on* (left alone) has been used. There is a series of names combining words meaning male and female: *junak žena, ćovek žena maška žena, muška devojka, momak devojka, momak djevojka, djevojka momak,* (these six using 'boy girl' or 'girl boy', 'man woman' or 'man girl'; some of these minor differences are only dialectic). In some cases 'sworn virgins' are indicated by the use of a masculine term with a female name or a feminine term with a male name: *muška Petra, maška Petra* (man Petra [Petra is a female name]); *enski Petko,* (woman Petko [Petko is a male name]).

36. Post, S. E. P. (1998), *Women in Modern Albania*, Jefferson, North Carolina; London: McFarland, p. 57.

37. His account refers to the subject as Fatime who changed her name to the male Fetah; and the army to the Yugoslav partisans. Fetah reverted to the use of the name Fatime when she later married. Grémaux, R. (1989), 'Mannish Women of the Balkan Mountains,' in Bremmer, J. (ed.), *From Sappho to de Sade: Moments in the History of Sexuality*, London: Routledge, pp. 162–3.

38. Demick (1 July 1996), 'In Albania, a Girl Who Became a Man', *Philadelphia Inquirer*.

39. The work is described both in Elsie, R. (1995), *History of Albanian Literature*, Boulder, Colorado: East European Monographs, no. 379, pp. 650–1, and in Grémaux (1992) 'Franciscan Friars', p. 361.

40. Miller, E.C. (1929), *Pran of Albania*, Garden City, New York: Doubleday, Doran & Co. Inc.

41. Munro, A. (27 June–4 July 1994), 'The Albanian Virgin'. *New Yorker*, pp. 118–38; also published in A. Munro (1994), *Open Secrets*, New York: Chatto, pp. 81–128.

42. Personal interview in 1998 with Mimi Lacej, Albanian human rights worker, the only Albanian member of the team of election supervisors for the Organization for Security and Cooperation in Europe in the Bosnian elections, November, 1998; native of Shkodër.

5

Living as Men

This is the most extraordinary custom of mountain Albania: If a girl refuses to marry the bridegroom chosen by her parents, to whom she may have been betrothed before birth, she must shear her head and turn herself as far as possible into a male. Sexless as an anchorite, she is expected to take part in tribal wars. Masculine labor is demanded of her. In a blood feud, she takes the same part as her brothers, but if she has a lover, it is the man whom she ought to have married who must avenge her chastity. We had one such girl with our caravan. She was an excellent shot. For weeks I thought she was a man.

Rosita Forbes, *Gypsy in the Sun*[1]

We have established the existence of 'sworn virgins' in Albania, their purpose and their whereabouts, we have defined their many terms and considered their roles in film and fiction, it is appropriate to recount the very varied histories of some of the remarkable women. These are women who have chosen, been permitted and encouraged by their society or even parentally predestined, to become men.

During the past decade, I have been able to spend time with a number of these women who have remained dedicated to their decision although in several cases only sketchy details were obtainable (it was not always convenient or possible to make detailed interviews).

Each case is entirely different, not only because of the family structure to which they belong, but also to the interpretation put on own her role as 'sworn virgin', and adaptation to the situation surrounding her. In most cases neither the transition to life as a male, nor the carrying out of it, fits exactly into the rules set out in previous chapters. The most important indicator of whether or not we can perceive any given 'sworn virgin' as such, lies in the acceptance of them by all within their very traditional home settings, rural (more usually) or urban. The situation of the rural 'virgins' would appear to fit more closely the traditional role while the 'virgins' in the towns seem to have adapted to more modern mores. Another characteristic of the rural 'virgins' is that all those whom I met were still living in the home of their birth.

In order to discover how each individual fitted the role of 'sworn virgin', I tried to elicit responses to a wide variety of queries, both from the individuals

Figure 18. Pashke harvesting beans. AY: Okolo, 1994

themselves and from those with whom they interacted closely. Almost everywhere I was greeted with enthusiasm and extreme hospitality and graciousness, my questions were seriously considered, giving me a picture of the wide variety of their lives which I record below. I was interested to find out how the 'sworn virgins' had taken on their role, whether it had involved any ritual event, whether their families had initiated, encouraged or discouraged the change, how their own lives had changed and how they themselves perceived their role in society. However, as mentioned elsewhere discussion concerning sexuality was usually very hard to initiate.

In view of the wide differences we shall look first at the rural cases and then observe some urban ones, which indicate a changing trend. In some, alternative names have been given to the 'virgins' to preserve anonymity. However, this has not been necessary in all cases as most are extremely proud of their transformation and social position. The findings of other researchers and press reports during the 1990s are incorporated, since almost all of them refer to one or more of the 'sworn virgins' whom I had already interviewed.

Rural 'Sworn Virgins'

Lule

Lule and her family live in a single-storey house in a little village some thirty miles from Shkodër and not far from the Adriatic coast, rather more easily accessible than most of the 'virgins' whom I visited. The pathway to reach her home is impassable by motorized vehicle and is often muddy from its use by cows and other animals which pass by. The house is set back from this pathway, up several deep concrete steps. On arrival at Lule's home there is always a hearty welcome for visitors. Chickens around the entrance scatter as the whole family emerges; all the adults present at the time, along with a crowd of barefoot children, display lively curiosity combined with an immediate desire to offer hospitality. Visitors are enthusiastically ushered inside. It takes a while to adjust to the contrasting darkness; the small windows are heavily curtained, and the dark pink walls add to the enveloping atmosphere, as we enter the heart of the home. Lule takes visitors into the *oda*: as this is a Catholic home there are settees rather than floor rugs to sit on, and a collection of religious artifacts displayed on a small table. By contrast an imitation tapestry decoration featuring a stag with a mountainous backdrop covers most of one wall.

Lule commands the women to see that visitors are served food and drink. One of the daughters of the household, Dafina, a young teenager, eagerly takes on her task; her mother is preoccupied with two small children. She brings trays of cool drinks and sweet Turkish coffee served in tiny cups and places them all neatly on the white hand-made lace table-cloth. She is extremely attentive to the needs of all present. All the other children are kept out of the room. Lule's older sister Drane (not married due to her ill-health), sits on the floor, whereas Lule sits on a settee. Drane wears traditional clothing: headscarf, a full white blouse and a full dark skirt with white apron, while the younger women and children are all dressed in Western-style clothing. On later visits we were taken into the back room where Drane was bedridden for several months before she died (in 1997).

Lule was the tenth child in a family of eleven. After seven daughters, her mother gave birth to twin boys, one of whom died shortly after. From all accounts Pjetar, the surviving twin, was thoroughly spoiled by the whole family, even smothered by his parents and seven older sisters. Growing up in this protected environment it became clear that he could not accept his responsibilities as the only son in a family with nine daughters. Lule remembers only ever having behaved as a boy and spent her time as an equal with the boys in primary school. Her older sister Drane says 'we tried to dress Lule in skirts, but she always refused. And we made such a fuss of Pjetar when he was little: he became incapable of doing anything for himself.' Lule always knew she didn't want to marry: 'I used to run away when I was a child if I heard that anyone was coming to try to arrange my marriage.' It became increasingly obvious that Pjetar was incompetent[2] to become the head of the household and representative at village meetings 'and in any case he had always accepted me as a brother', said Lule. On the death of their parents only a year after Pjetar married, when Lule was about nineteen, she naturally took the household leadership. Now she heads her family of ten (when I first met her) and runs a small business with her own welding machine. She never regretted her choice:

> I wouldn't have it otherwise ... here I am in control, I have a large family. We have enough land for us all to live from when it is properly managed, I enjoy taking charge of going to market and trading our produce for household necessities. I take pride in managing the home, the family and the land as my father did before. I promised each of my parents, when they were dying, that I would ensure that the family was not dishonoured (i.e. that the family would not break up just because her brother was not a capable manager). Work is the most important thing in my life, though I do miss the company of my workmates from the days when I was a tractor driver (in the Communist period).

Pjetar's wife confirmed the need for Lule as head of a household: 'I did find the situation odd when I was first married,' she admitted, 'but I soon got used to it, and now Lule is like a brother to me.' Pjetar does little to help in the family who all look to Lule for both outside income and family decision-making and the management of their several dynyms of land.[3] He does not appear to resent the teasing he receives even from the children of the family who say that all he does is sleep. A visiting aunt is full of praise for Lule, commenting on what an important role she has played in keeping the family together and running the household so efficiently despite difficult times. It is

Figure 19. Lule (in dark glasses) heads a family of ten. The woman closest to her, to her right, is her sister (deceased 1997). AY: Velipoje, 1994

Lule who does all the chopping, planting and mowing to produce the animal feed they sell.

When discussing her youth, Lule showed me photographs of herself as a boy amongst other schoolboys; later photos depict her as a young man, driving tractors and trucks – her occupation since the age of fourteen, and attending weddings in smart masculine attire (suit with waistcoat and tie, the trousers with neatly pressed flares). As an observer well accustomed to seeing women in trousers, it is particularly her firm, assertive stance that stands out for me. Sometimes Lule wears her black leather men's jacket and in summer men's sunglasses. She wears other simple male accoutrements like her men's wristwatch (rarely worn by women). It is also her ready swigging of alcohol, her grasping for cigarettes, her lighting of others', as well as her total control of every group situation in which I met and observed her, which confirm the ease with which she fulfills the role of family head.

Such masculinity appears especially exaggerated alongside the feminine attire and comparatively reticent behaviour of the village women wearing headscarves and dressed in full skirts with aprons; to Albanians, Lule is certainly seen as a man.

Lule revels in her position, slapping the backs of those men she considers her friends. Clearly she commands deference of everyone, male and female

Figure 20. Lule (on the right), socializing: simple accoutrements like her man's wristwatch, her sunglasses (never worn by peasant women). AY: Velipoje, 1994

with whom she comes into contact, both in her village and further afield. We made expeditions out of her immediate home vicinity and I was interested to observe that she was still accorded the same respect usual only to the presence of a man of considerable stature.

On one visit to Lule, she was already entertaining a male visitor. On our arrival she demanded that her friend, Artan, send one of the children to fetch his new bride to meet us. After a time she arrived accompanied by her mother-in-law; she was dressed in her long white modern bridal gown and wore bright red lipstick, rouged cheeks and a mass of mascara. Her finely coiffed hair was partially visible under a white wedding veil and children held a longer veil and the dress of her skirt to keep it from the muddy path as she approached Lule's home. Once in the house we saw that she was wearing high-heeled stiletto shoes. She nervously entered the *oda* for us to admire, and sat awkwardly without saying a word for the remainder of our visit.

Pjetar's six remaining children live in Lule's household (four having died at birth or in infancy) – some of them have asked 'why do we call Lule "aunt" when she's a man?' Asked whether she missed having a sex life, Lule responded firmly that five minutes of pleasure is certainly not worth all the

Figure 21. Lule doing maintenance work on her welding machine. AY: Velipoje, 1994

mess and squalor of a resulting baby.[4] It is clear that Lule has kept strictly to her vow of celibacy in order to maintain the authority which honour demands.

Dilore

Dilore also lived in the lowlands in another small village amidst lush cultivated smallholdings. I was taken to meet this 84-year-old who presided over the Bujari household. 'She still commands extraordinary respect from all around, though no longer able to take the active role she fulfilled during most of her life,' her nephew Gjoke told me. At the age of six, while walking in the woods, Dile met a herbal doctor from whom she learnt the properties of the local plants. She applied herbal remedies from then on, and doctors from the local hospital and further afield came to seek her advice. She claimed to have a six-day herbal cure for hepatitis, and another made from a root which grows in the woods nearby, effective for certain eye complaints.[5] By the age of eight, with two sisters and no brothers, Dile changed her name (to Dilore) and made the decision to become a boy, never to marry, but to gain the advantages of a man's life. She called a meeting of all her relatives, and despite their lack of enthusiasm concerning her choice, Dilore stood by it and soon earned the respect both of her family and of all their neighbours. On the

Figure 22. Dilore 1994 (deceased 1996). AY: village outside Shkodër, 1994

death of her mother several years later, Dilore's father remarried and had a son, Nikoll, but this did not affect Dilore's decision.[6] Later when their parents died, Dilore and Nikoll built their own house. Nikoll married, his son also married, and the household consisted of seven.

Dilore refused to perform military service or even the compulsory training as she strongly disapproved of the Communist government. When I last met her, she was still the representative at village meetings. During the Communist era this family was one of the last to relinquish their land, which was eventually taken by force. Dilore, a devout Catholic, often received police visits on this account, but held her own in these potential confrontations: 'I knew how to talk to these men, sometimes I bribed them; I made sure my family gave them traditional hospitality but in the end it was officials from outside the region who finally confiscated our land.'[7] Nikoll recalls: 'they didn't dare arrest Dilore, he was held in such high regard by the whole village'. She was frequently asked to represent the village as 'headman' in the *dashmor*, a traditional custom of fetching a bride to her wedding, for which Dilore would wear a *xhamadan* (embroidered ceremonial marriage waistcoat worn by men on these occasions). Dilore was especially known for her wise land management and ability to make sufficient profits to give produce and money to the village community.

Gjoke's wife found it strange when she first married into the household, but acquiesced: 'it's my responsibility to work for Dilore, even if she is at times whimsical'. Many comment on but accept her use of strong swear words, deemed appropriate only for men. Dilore (whose male attire is of traditional style, including the white 'skull cap') frequently walked considerable distances to visit people in surrounding areas. On our visits she was often absent visiting other men in the neighbourhood. Dilore told a story of a man who once challenged what might be uncovered below her belt: 'I pointed my gun at him and threatened to kill him; he finished up pleading for his life!'[8] She used to enjoy amusing her friends by making advances towards outsider girls who didn't know her true sex, but revealed the truth as they became uneasy at her advances. Nikoll, responding to questions concerning Dilore's sexuality mentioned that 'as he said himself, he used to enjoy teasing attractive young girls, but it would have been out of the question for him to have carried the joke any further – what else could he have done?' As a 'sworn virgin' there was no question that Dilore could pursue any possible inclinations further. Dilore's greatest regret is that: 'the Communists took away my horse and my gun'.

Pashke

Orphaned at a year old, Pashke lives with her invalid uncle in a remote mountain village where she was brought up by her grandmother and uncle.[9] Shortly after her grandmother's death when Pashke was eighteen, her uncle was taken to hospital in Shkodër fifty miles away. The petite Pashke made the journey twice each month for seven months to visit her uncle in hospital, walking most of the mountainous way.

Although Pashke had never met a 'sworn virgin', she knew of her traditional right according to the *Kanun* laws. 'To dress as a man earns the respect of a man,' she explained. In order to prepare for the long journeys Pashke made the decision to forsake life as a woman:

Figure 23. Pashke with her uncles. AY: Okolo, 1993

A girl alone could not undertake such journeys. I did not have long to think through what I did. I took some of my uncle's clothes, my own in any case were only fit for rags. It was a time of such distress that I didn't discuss it with anyone, just acted as I had to, and cannot see now that I could have done otherwise. I have done in my life whatever has been necessary and this has been my fate.

Pashke had been a Commune worker under Communism. On his return from hospital, her uncle could only respond with gratitude to his niece who now works on their tiny smallholding of terraced fields, tending the crops of beans, potatoes and corn from which they manage to eke out a living. Her musta-chioed uncle says of her 'she's been the son I never had – I couldn't have managed without her' and a female neighbour comments 'they are a very correct household, Pashke and her uncle, but I do not relate to Pashke as a woman. I think of her as a man.' Pashke admits to being lonely, spending most of her time with this uncle and another elderly uncle. Social outings are few in the village, but Pashke smokes and drinks with the men at weddings, funerals and occasional village meetings (whereas a woman's role at such functions is to serve and then to leave). As Pashke's uncle is old and frail, she remains as the head and as such the inheritor of the home. There are no women in Pashke's household, she therefore also carries out the household duties and keeps the little house with two tiny rooms and its minimal contents, clean and tidy. In order to perform traditional duties in entertaining guests, Pashke makes coffee in the hearth, but whereas a woman would serve it with *raki* (strong local brandy) and leave, she serves it and sits with her uncles and the guests and shares cheerily in the toasts and discussion. Ending my first visit, with my departure on foot, Pashke accompanied me to the boundaries of the village: this was the extent of her responsibility for my protection under the age-old laws of hospitality (see Figure 13).[10]

Shkurtan

Shkurtan's village, at the end of a deeply rutted ten-kilometre track hewn out of rock, is singularly unusual in that it has been home to no less than five 'sworn virgins' in the last fifty years. The village, sheltered all round by sandstone mountains, straggles along the valley floor, the houses at distances just visible from one another. At night, as in other villages everyone stays inside their homes after dark when the dogs are set loose: a threat to the life of any intruder to the village.

Shkurtan, now in her seventies, is the oldest of the 'virgins' still alive whom I met. At a young age, on the death of an older brother, Shkurtan's parents decided that one of their twin daughters should take his place, and from that moment treated Shkurtan as a boy. 'I didn't want to marry and have someone else rule over me – it's me who rules' she says assertively, happy that all refer to her as a man. She even masculinized her name by adding 'n' to her previously female name (Shkurta). Shkurtan is a Muslim though there is no mosque in the village.

She now lives with Bute, her brother's widow, in the family home, with a wooden tiled roof; the ground floor is a storage barn, the living space above. The house is situated just above the valley floor and is surrounded by small lush cornfields. In front of the house is a small tended apple and plum orchard.

Figure 24. Shkurtan rolls her own cigarette. AY: village outside Bajram Curri, 1994

Shkurtan owns two cows, and at the time of my summer visits was constantly busy with preparations for winter: harvesting hay and corn, and chopping wood. Bute as a widow when her mother-in-law died leaving Shkurtan without domestic help, was the obvious person to take over this domestic role. When receiving visitors, while Shkurtan was out in the fields, Bute provided generous hospitality, bringing trays of fresh creamy milk, yoghurt, Turkish coffee in little handleless cups, *raki*, and platters of apples and plums,

Figure 25. Shkurtan with her sister-in-law, Bute who says 'I felt sorry for him, and it was also a family decision that he needed a woman to take care of him and the home' (after Shkurtan's mother died). AY: village outside Bajram Curri, 1994

placing them on a white cloth on the grass for us. On these occasions, Bute did not sit in the circle with the visitors, but sat away from the group, always watching, ready to provide replenishment. Bute talked caringly of Shkurtan:

> I came to live with him, rather than with any of my six children or eight grand-children. I couldn't leave him without help; I felt sorry for him, and it was also a family decision that he needed a woman to take care of him and the home. I only go away to visit my children and grandchildren for one or two nights at a time at

Figure 26. Shkurtan and Haki assist with neighbours' corn harvest. Note contrasting clothing of the two women in the centre of the picture, the two 'sworn virgins' at either edge, and the one man. AY: village outside Bajram Curri, 1994

most, and even then I leave everything in the house ready for him – he only does men's work. There is much to be done with the cows, twenty chickens as well as various crops. He does none of the domestic chores.

Whereas Bute has soft skin and her pale face is framed by a white headscarf, it is hard to recognize any female features in Shkurtan's physique. She is rarely seen without her man's flat cap. Her stride is heavy and masculine, her handshake very firm and her stance authoritative. Her face is very weathered, her large hands are very rough and her chest appears to be completely flat. Shkurtan has no time for chatter and is not very forthcoming on personal issues preferring to discuss the productivity of her land in which she takes great pride. She comments on the difficulties of plowing without any machinery, and using only very crude forms of irrigation which need constant attention. She chops wood to feed the cooking stove and checks the progress of her corn crop. She appears to be much more at ease with her male visitors, sitting with them on a bench, than with Bute and women guests seated on the ground.

Figure 27. Haki with her one cow. AY: village outside Bajram Curri, 1994

Haki

Sometimes Shkurtan would take us to visit Haki, another of the virgins from the village who lives alone in her own house. At such times, Shkurtan always insisted on carrying my rucksack. Both Haki and Shkurtan dress in male attire. They roll their own cigarettes, drink *raki* and socialize with men of the village – all activities from which village women are traditionally excluded. Haki's masculine appearance is enhanced by her particularly deep voice as well as by a cigarette which is usually seen, tucked behind her ear. On asking whether Haki ever feels lonely, she replies: 'On such occasions I go to visit relatives [who live several hours' distance away], but I don't feel any happier, and just want to get home.' Other villagers speak highly of both Shkurtan and Haki who are proud of their positions and both claim that their greatest concern is to lead honest and respected lives. Both of them take their turns in helping their neighbours at times of special need, especially harvesting, and receive reciprocal assistance. Although she has no family nearby, Haki has nephews in the nearest town who come to stay during the summer months. They will eventually inherit her home. Both Haki and Shkurtan have the means to protect themselves in case of attack and affirm that they would be ready to avenge family honour by taking a life if it became necessary. This is the duty only of men. They are fully aware of the laws of the *Kanun*.

When I asked Bute about Shkurtan's sexuality and sexual preference, she replied: 'He has no sexual interest, even though he used to be very attractive.' Haki felt similarly: 'I've always been like an old woman, without sexual feelings.' As with most of the 'sworn virgins' I met, Shkurtan herself was reticent in discussing her sexuality.

Rafadam

For a decade the photographer, Lala Meredith-Vula, has regularly visited Rafadam (nicknamed Raba), a shepherd living in a village in the Rugova mountains of Kosov@. When she first visited in 1990, Raba was already elderly and was living with her brother's family in the lowlands in the area of Peć. In the summers the family moves to the mountain pastures, where Raba spends most of her time. She leads a solitary life with her flock of sheep: she knows each one's age, and has given them all names. When Meredith-Vula wished to photograph the shepherd together with her scattered sheep, Raba made a high-pitched whistle and the sheep obediently came to her, trying to touch her, almost knocking her down as they came.

Raba is accepted as a man in the community without question and eats with the men while women serve them. Only close neighbours and family know her true identity. She is an old man in most people's eyes. Her story was so painful to her that her nephew Agim Qarraj told it to Meredith-Vula, explaining that Raba is quiet and honourable but doesn't discuss her situation with anyone.

Raba was born in 1920 in Rugova and was betrothed to marry a neigh-bouring village family's son at a very young age. The fathers had arranged the suit. When she was sixteen her fiancé was tragically murdered in a shoot-out in the hills, against Montenegrin bandits. She was devastated as this made her ineligible ever to marry. Were she to do so, this would instantly dishonour both her family and the memory of her dead fiancé, giving cause to the fiancé's family to take blood revenge on her own, according to the

Kanun, Agim explained. When she was seventeen Raba's father decided to make her a *tybeli* (their term for 'sworn virgin'), which she has remained ever since.

Meredith-Vula's many conversations with Raba were about her sheep and living in the mountains. The winters are the hardest times as she hates being confined indoors in their home on the plains. In summer she roams the mountains which she says is the only life she knows and that she would never want to exchange it.

Meredith-Vula last visited Raba's family in March 1998, but was only able to speak to Agim as Raba had already left for the mountains. The family were planning soon to follow and to stay there through the coming harsh winter rather than risk the dangerous political situation which had evolved, in the plains of Peć, where many of the surrounding villages have already been burned by the Serbs. They will not even risk going to check on whether their house is still standing.

Selman

Back across the border from Kosov@, in the less threatened area of northern Albania, Fatos Baxhaku interviewed Sema in the village of Lepurush in 1996.[11] Barbara Demick reported on Selman Brahimi (the same person).[12] Selman has lived as a man since her father died when she was thirteen. A third reporter, Freedman also visited her:

> Selman Brahim strides through the house with a confident swagger. He proffers cigarettes, then orders a young woman to make the coffee and bring *raki*. Visitors are rare in this remote village in rugged northern Albania and Selman, as head of the family, takes obvious pride in this rare opportunity to display his hospitality . . . his hands are rough, his back straight, his hair short, his face lined and slightly suspicious. He wears heavy boots, thick trousers and a white shirt that is grubby around the cuffs. It's the shirt that gives him away; it seems curiously cut, tight in the wrong places; which of course it is. It was cut for a man, and Selman Brahim is a woman.[13]

Demick's interview gives much more detailed information. Sema, of a Muslim family, was one of four daughters. They live in the remote village with a population of 300 but not a single telephone, automobile or house with indoor plumbing. The village women wear long skirts, aprons and white head scarves. A son, Elez, was born shortly before her father's death, but it would be far too long to wait for him to head the household. So Sema masculinized her name to Selman and thereafter her mother and sisters used masculine pronouns when referring to her. She did not notify any government agencies of her change since the only effect would have been a military call-up.[14] Of much greater importance is that all who know her recognize her special status and the fact that she respects the local law. She learned to play two musical instruments, only played by men, the *fyell* (a kind of flute) and the *lahutë* (stringed instrument).[15] When her brother was old enough to work, her mother suggested that Selman should revert to being a woman and get married; however she said that once something is decided, it cannot be changed and that in any case she considered herself a man. As household head, she selected a wife, Hasije, for her brother and, suitably attired, took the role of groom's father at his wedding. Hasije who has borne four sons and refers to Selman as her brother-in-law, is now responsible for all the housework for the six men.

Sokol

We met the petite Sokol by chance, in passing. She was riding a pony alongside a road outside Bajram Curri, accompanied by her nephew Gjovalin on foot. Sokol had changed her name from Zhirë when a young girl. Gjovalin has a wife and three sons, but Sokol heads this household. We never would have recognized that Sokol was a woman in her traditional white closely fitting felt 'skull cap', waistcoat, man's shirt and loose brown trousers; we were introduced by locals with whom we were travelling.[16]

Drane

Julius Strauss interviewed Drane Popaj and learned that she was born into a family with two daughters and one son. She had made her decision to become a man in the 1920s when the Serbs invaded northern Albania; she felt that a family with only one son was very vulnerable.[17]

Urban 'Sworn Virgins'

The role of household head for urban 'sworn virgins' is less obvious than for those in rural environments. Their occupations, unlike the agricultural activity of the rural 'virgins', do not demand the overseeing of a self-sufficient production unit. However, on closer investigation it is clearly evident that their gender role gives them equal status with urban household heads.

I met 'sworn virgins' in the very contrasting towns of Shkodër, and Bajram Curri. Shkodër is the economic and cultural capital of northern Albania with Illyrian origins and a long history as an intellectual centre for Albanians. Bajram Curri is a small new town far from any mainstream culture; it has just two asphalted streets and most of its Communist-built multi-storey apartment blocks stand on littered wasteland. This barren, isolated town is

Figure 28. Sanie with the truck which she's driven during Communist and post-Communist times. AY: Bajram Curri, 1994

surrounded by mountains and is extremely difficult to reach. It is often likened to the United States 'Wild West', and especially lived up to this reputation during the extreme crisis in Kosov@ in 1998–99.

Sanie

It was in this town that I met Sanie, thirty-six years old at the time. She heads an all-female household comprised of her mother and sisters. Sanie's mother had two stillborn sons; when Sanie survived, her parents were so delighted that they wanted her to be a boy and brought her up as one, although relatives outside her immediate family disapproved. No further sons were born. Sanie completed seven years of school and became a truck driver and road maintenance worker. She was proud to have worked eighteen years at the same job that she had under Communism, driving the same old Russian truck. Now she is in partnership with the man who was previously her boss and who treats her as his equal: 'I consider Sanie a fine and reliable person, neither man nor woman.' When I asked her about the implications of her decision to remain celibate, Sanie laughed: 'I made the choice, there's no way I could turn back now. Besides, I enjoy being free to travel.'

Medi

Medi, the youngest 'sworn virgin' was twenty-two when I first met her. She lives in the small town of Bajram Curri, in an isolated area surrounded by mountains, into which thousands of Kosovar refugees have since fled. On our first meeting she was very uneasy and reticent regarding her situation. To me she appeared to be the kind of modern young woman you might find anywhere in the world. She was dressed in a pastel jumper and lurid emerald shiny shellsuit trousers. I did however recognize that none of the other young women in this very remote small town wore anything more unusual than cotton skirts, even if they had abandoned the aprons and headscarves of older women. Medi is slim with short, cropped, dark hair, and she plays football (unheard of for girls in this area). She is the youngest of three sisters in a relatively poor family. Their father is a policeman nearing retirement. At this time Medi seemed to be coming to terms with her role but was somewhat reticent in discussing her situation.

When I visited Medi a year later she had completed her first year of a three-year course at a police training college in Tirana, preparing to follow in her father's footsteps in the police force (unprecedented for women at that time). She had lived and worked primarily amongst men. Now she walked with self-confidence and greeted us lustily. As we walked together she turned her head now and then to spit on the ground, an action rarely observed among women. She was dressed in black jeans and a black denim jacket and was wearing trainers. Her step, now a stride, had gained the assurance of a man with purpose. She walked, with her hands in her pockets, alone in the streets (also unheard of for young women in such a tradition-oriented town) and frequented cafes to smoke and drink with men. Hosting us at a cafe, Medi shouted her order for coffee and *raki*; she smoked continuously during this meeting. More recently she is talking of emigrating (as do so many young men who seek jobs and thus money to send home to their families).

Still looking at the phenomena of 'sworn virgins' in urban settings, I met and interviewed four further women in the towns of northern Albania, all living as men, but failed to find a fifth whose story I had heard.

Hajdar

Hajdar (Harry), in her sixties when we met in 1995, now lives in Bajram Curri. She changed her name from Fatime as a teenager. She became a household head when her brother was killed, leaving a wife and six children. Now she still enjoys all the privileges as household head of this, her youngest nephew's family. Hajdar is deeply insulted if anyone refers to her as a woman, all her relatives call her 'uncle'.

Xhema

Xhemalija or Xhema, also in her sixties when we met in 1996, lives in Shkodër and is known as 'Xhema the mechanic'. She told me she was one of six children, that one brother died as a child, and two of her sisters before they reached adulthood. Brought up as a boy from birth, she dresses and looks like a man. She worked first as a mechanic repairing bicycles and later got a job as ticket officer at a Bingo club which was recently installed in a disused cinema. She now lives with a younger brother and his wife, and behaves as an uncle to her two sisters' children, living nearby. There is another account in which the name change occurs on the death of her father when she was sixteen. This version tells of the fury of her brother when she cut her hair and insisted on acting as a boy.[18]

Liljana

In Shkodër also, I met Liljana, wearing a pinstripe man's suit. She currently heads her parents' household. Liljana was born in Bulgaria to Albanian parents in 1957. Her father was a loyal Communist official who worked in the Albanian Embassy in Sofia until the breakdown of relations between the two countries by 1960. At the time of their return to Albania, Liljana was one of four daughters (there were no sons). Never disclosing in the interview whether she took the oath, she simply stated that she used the name Lil and took a man's role. She worked as a supervisor of machinery in Shkodër's tobacco factory (a job normally given to men) until the fall of Communism, when the factory closed down.[19] Her sisters have all married and emigrated to Italy. Lil is now unemployed.

Lindita

Lindita, also living in Shkodër, in her forties, was the most feminine-looking of all our interviewees. It was hard to imagine how others could perceive such a buxom woman as a man despite the fact that she was wearing a man's short-sleeved shirt, trousers, a man's watch and used many masculine mannerisms. She chain-smoked and gesticulated assertively as she told us of her difficult life. Her father died when she was four years old. By the age of ten, having no other sibs, Lindita saw the necessity of taking a male role for her mother's sake. She worked as an electrical engineer for several years. There were problems at work and she became antagonistic towards certain Party members. Her anger culminated in her taking a picture of the then leader, Enver Hoxha, and smashing it in front of local Party members during a meeting. Such defiance earned Lindita a twelve-year prison sentence. She served only five years as the regime fell while she was in prison and she was freed. During those five years, Lindita served in the men's prison and was the subject of extreme abuse. She mentioned that her teeth were kicked in, but did not go into greater detail. Under the new Democratic government, Lindita and her mother were eligible for state assistance earmarked for those who had suffered persecution from the previous government. Their need is especially great as their home has been claimed by a previous owner (the descendant of an owner from fifty years before). However, no assistance has so far been forthcoming; the disastrous collapse of the 'pyramid' schemes in 1997 affected all such monetary promises. Lindita has not been able to find employment; her mother is sick and nearly blind. Lindita is now keen to see if there is any way she can emigrate; she is willing to work hard, long hours if only she could find work.

Angelina

In a similar vein, another 'sworn virgin' who suffered under Communism was Angjelina. She had been married during the Communist era, but shortly afterwards was imprisoned for political reasons. On her release many years later, she had no home, was unable to find her husband or family, and felt the only solution was to become a man (Luk) in order to exist by staying with various families wherever she could find one to take her in. Whereas it would not be fitting for a woman to be asking such a favour, it was acceptable for a man to do so.

Factors in Common

All the 'sworn virgins' I met spoke very positively about their changed gender, seeing it as the best functional way to integrate into their specific family where the kin-group had been unacceptably lacking in male leadership. Only Pashke voiced a tentative regret: 'I am sorry for others who lead this kind of life. I had no other option, given my circumstances. I cannot go back on my decision,' she said. It is so great a source of prestige to lead a man's life that none of them felt at any disadvantage, despite their choice inevitably resulting in a renunciation of sexuality, marriage and childbearing. Stuart Freedman asked a similar question of Selman Brahim who replied, 'Is there any man who decided to be a woman? Of course not. No, the man is more privileged everywhere.'[20]

Of the 'sworn virgins' mentioned in this chapter, ranging in age from 22–85, I am only aware of the death of one (Dilore, in 1995). She lived, as the others all do, in northern Albania, with the exception of the Kosovar, Rafadam. Other than these two, three live in the town of Shkodër, three in the much smaller town of Bajram Curri in the eastern mountains, and most of the others in remote mountain villages, only accessible with great difficulty. Only Lule lives in the lowlands, near the coast, where she has received several reporters.

The reasons given for these women becoming men were primarily to fill a male role where there was no other man available. Only one (Rafadam) gave as a reason anything relating to a broken engagement (her fiancé was killed). The choice was made by parents at birth or early childhood in three cases (Shkurtan, Medi and Xhemlija). Of the others, three made their own choice in childhood (Lule, Dilore and Lindita), and most of the rest as teenagers, except for Selman and Angelina (whose changed situation in later life led them to make the decision).

Rafadam, Xhema and Medi (the youngest) are the only ones who are not heads of households, though Medi is preparing to take on that role. Rural household heads had a clearly defined role, organizing their self-sufficient family units. Inevitably the average size of families headed by 'sworn virgins' is smaller than the national average family size: larger families would be likely to have a qualified male to take the leadership role. In this matter Lule is an exception (heading, before her sister's death, a family of ten).

Several of the urban 'virgins' head a household of only one, but this still gives them the legitimacy to live alone, to own their home and to interact with men and with households in the wider community as persons whose advice may be sought and acted upon. Their occupations are varied, whereas all those from rural environments are involved in agriculture. Religion does not apparently play an important part in the lives of most of the 'sworn virgins' whom I met. None had made their oath before religious leaders. Dilore was the most devout (Catholic); Lule displays pictures of saints in her home, but does not have strong links with the Church. Shkurtan and Haki gave as an excuse for their inactivity and disinterest as Muslims, the fact that there is no mosque either in or near their village. The only references to the Orthodox faith relates to 'sworn virgins' in Montenegro, one of Grémaux's cases had an Orthodox burial, the other was Stefan in the film *Virdžina*. The religions of northern Albania are Muslim and Catholic, the Orthodox population live primarily in southern Albania. Under Communism, all religious activity was forbidden from 1967, religious leaders were persecuted, tortured and many killed. Albania was proclaimed an atheist state for twenty-three years until 1990; during that time all religious buildings were closed, demolished or turned to other uses. The usual response of indifference to my enquiries concerning religious affiliation probably reflects the effect of living so many years under Communism. The strict form of Communism in Albania directly affected at least four of the 'sworn virgins' (Dilore, Pashke, Lindita and Angelina). It may be that other 'sworn virgins' who were strongly religious were exiled and prevented from taking their leadership role.

It is apparently age which dictates the kind of men's clothing which the 'virgins' wear – two of the oldest (Dilore and Sokol) both wore an adaptation of the traditional men's wear shown in Edith Durham's picture (Figure 1). They both wore 'skull caps' and trousers, baggy around the hips, together with Western-style men's jackets, shirts and machine-made boots. Had Durham's 'virgin' been wearing shoes she would have worn hand-made *opangi* (sandals made of roughly dried hide). All the other 'sworn virgins' wear clothes which we would recognize as male attire, often including such additional male accoutrements as leather belts, sunglasses and men's wrist watches. Only Medi dresses in clothing which could be interpreted as fashionable, following new Western styles only available since the fall of Communism.

Medi presents exceptions in several areas: she is the only one to have received further education, or to have spent extended periods away from her family (whilst training in Tirana). Furthermore she was the only one who showed any indication of ambivalence concerning her role (at our first meeting), though subsequently this ambivalence was no longer evident, possibly indicating that it takes time to fully adjust to gender change, especially under the social instability in post-Communist Albania.

Among the factors that all these women share are economic hardship and a strength of character. Most live without any contact with others like them, yet they all observe the *Kanun*'s demand that an honourable home is headed by a man. They live in a strictly patriarchal society where women's roles are completely subservient, yet they have convincingly made a break from that role both in dress, behaviour and self-assertion. As far as I could ascertain they all live celibate lives, most accepting that this is part of the inevitable situation which their choice has brought them, and none voicing any regret concerning that aspect of their lives (note particularly Lule's response, p. 71).

Despite the very different situations of each of the individuals observed in this chapter, I found them all to be totally accepted and even revered within their communities. They are united by their determination to stick with the oath (whether proclaimed or not) to live as men.

Notes

1. Forbes, R. (1944), *Gypsy in the Sun*, New York: E.P. Dutton & Co. inc., p. 192.

2. Facchia explained Pjetar's deficiency in terms of impaired speech and hearing, Facchia, L. (date unknown) in *DS*, translated into Albanian (20 Oct. 1998), 'Virgjëreshat e Shndërruara në Burra' (Virgins Transformed into Men), *Shekulli*, p. 19.

3. One dynym is approximately one thousand square metres.

4. Lule has received several reporters since my first visit to her in 1994. Steve Pagani wrote up her story which appeared first in the United States, then in Australia in 1996 (3–5 June), '"Vowed Virgins" Keep Countryside Under Control', *Illyria*, p. 4. (7 May 1996), 'Albania's "Avowed Virgins" Wear the Trousers', *Guardian*; Tom Parfitt visited Lule and Pashke, and reported their stories in a Scottish newspaper (1 June 1997), 'Land Beyond Time' *Spectrum*, p. 2; Julius Strauss talked to Lule and confirmed all that I had found, in his report: (6 Feb. 1997), 'The Virgins Who Live Like Men and Treat Women as Inferior', the *Daily Telegraph*, p. 15. See also footnote 2. For details of Laura Facchia's article in 1998.

5. Barbara Kerewsky-Halpern points out that Dilore's status as a male may have made her an acceptable provider of cures, where a pre-menopausal woman would not be considered ritually clean.

6. As Mildred Dickemann notes: 'Thus preservation of the patriline could be achieved by the mature virgin's ascendancy during the immaturity of a later-born son': Dickemann, M. (1997), 'The Balkan Sworn Virgin: a Traditional European Transperson' in Bullough V. and B. and Elias, J., (eds), *Gender Blending*, Amherst, New York: Prometheus, p. 251.

7. The Catholics were the religious group who were the most severely persecuted as they were seen to be under the control of foreign agents, the Vatican at their head. This was used as justification for appropriating all Catholic property. Shkodër had been Albania's centre for Catholicism since the split from Eastern Orthodoxy in 1054.

The largest Catholic cathedral in the Balkans is located there; under Hoxha, it was used as a sports hall.

8. A similar story is told of the 'sworn virgin' Mikas: 'No one dared to mock him. Such a person, he declared convincingly, "pays with his head"'; Grémaux, R. (1994), 'Woman Becomes Man in the Balkans' in Herdt, G. (ed.), *Third Sex, Third Gender: Beyond Sexual Dimorphism in Culture and History*, New York: Zone Books, p. 247.

9. Facchia reports that Pashke is now about sixty years old. According to Facchia Pashke, as a child, saw Hoxha's soldiers kill the men of her family when they had tried to escape over the border out of Albania, and from that time she was brought up living in stables and without any female role model. Her childhood was spent with boys tending their sheep. As Pashke is now still in her forties, most of the above cannot hold true. Facchia (20 Oct. 1998), 'Virgjëreshat e Shndërruara në Burra'.

10. Tom Parfitt visited Lule and Pashke, and reported their stories in a Scottish newspaper: (1 June 1997), 'Land Beyond Time', p. 2.

11. Baxhaku, F. (21 May 1996), '"Ja përse Preferova të Jetoj si një Mashkull"' (Why I Prefer to Live as a Man), *Gazeta Shqiptare*, p. 7.

12. Demick, B. (1 July 1996), 'In Albania, a Girl Who Became a Man', *The Philadelphia Inquirer*.

13. Freedman (3 Nov. 1996) 'Self Made Men', *Independent on Sunday*, p. 14.

14. Modern Albanian governments have avoided recognition of the existence of traditions. After 1967, and especially after the 'cultural revolution' of 1974, many antiquated customs were declared non-existent. Hence there were no official records sought or kept of women living as men. Likewise in the new 'democracy' after 1992, to accept that traditional laws still prevailed in any area would acknowledge a degree of weakness of state power and public security.

15. Grémaux also comments on the playing of the *lahutë* as a privilege normally reserved for men, and features a photograph of the 'sworn virgin' Tonë in traditional clothing: a woollen hand-woven waistcoat, a striped sash at her waist and white woollen trousers with black braid down each leg, playing a *lahutë*. See: Grémaux (1994), 'Woman Becomes Man in the Balkans', p. 258.

16. One of our less successful attempts to meet a known 'sworn virgin' took us further up into the mountains in the remote region of Tropoje. Our two-hour journey along a dirt track from Bajram Curri and led us to a large village by the name of Tropoje. It has a spacious main square surrounded by houses with red-tiled rooves and whitewashed outside walls, and a single small shop. We had been told of Peçi, a 'sworn virgin' in her early thirties, and came here to visit her. We found her home, just off the main square. On arrival, however, the 'virgin' refused to meet us. The explanation from her family was that she was 'a little crazy'. We did not feel it appropriate to pursue the matter further.

17. Strauss (6 Feb. 1997), 'The Virgins Who Live Like Men', p. 15.

18. In *DS* (date unknown), translated into Albanian (20 Oct. 1998), 'Virgjëreshat e Shndërruara në Burra: Pashku, Lula dhe Xhema Tregojnë Historinë e Jetës së tyre' (Virgins Changed into Men: Pashke, Lule and Xhema Tell their Life Stories). Laura

Facchi, whose article on 'sworn virgins' first appeared in a French publication, reports that Xhema was offered a place on the men's ward when she was hospitalized. This was for breast cancer and when her true sex was discovered, she was given the choice of the men's or the women's ward, and chose the latter.

19. This is the only remaining state-owned factory and became Shkodër's main reception centre for Kosovar refugees in 1999.

20. Freedman (3 Nov. 1996), 'Self Made Men', p. 14.

6

Dress as a Signifier of Gender

Several differences in clothing were used to designate civil status. For example, a married woman could by no means dress any longer 'like a girl', and this expresses also the double function of clothing, both as a practical object and as a symbol. The same is expressed also by the clothing of 'virgins' ... In some zones they dressed entirely like men, whereas in others, partly in men's clothes, partly in women's clothes.

Andromaqi Gjergji, *Veshjet Shqiptare në Shekuj*
(Albanian Dress Through the Centuries)[1]

Definition and Classification of Dress

Eicher and Roach-Higgins' definition of 'dress' as gender-neutral has been used in this book to avoid the confusion associated with the 'clothing/ adornment dichotomy',[2] including those categories that go beyond what we would ordinarily define as 'dress' such as markings, and even mannerisms, if they do indeed proscribe a gender to the wearer. Eicher and Roach-Higgins use the word 'dress' as a 'comprehensive term to identify both direct body changes and items added to the body'. They consider that it is crucial for modern ethnographers to move away from the dichotomy mentioned above, that has influenced so much of the earlier research on this topic and stress the socio-cultural aspect of dress: 'that it is imbued with meaning understood by wearer and viewer. Having taken this sociocultural stance we define dress as an assemblage of body modifications and/or supplements displayed by a person in communicating with other human beings.'[3]

Looking back to the work of earlier behavioural sociologists and anthropologists, we see that such seemingly minor details as appearance and manner form an important part of character assessment within a given cultural context: 'In addition to the expected consistency between appearance and manner, we expect of course, some coherence among setting, appearance and manner. Such coherence presents an ideal type that provides us with a means of stimulating our attention to and interest in exceptions.'[4]

It is this definition of 'dress' that is applied to the phenomenon of the 'sworn virgins' as they have been described in this book. Clothing acts as a signifier in a society where dress is distinctively proscribed by gender. Make-up is very little used in traditional society except on festive occasions, whereas in the towns make-up is a mark of maturity. 'Sworn virgins', as men, never use any form of make-up. Neither do they ever, as the older women of this society do, dye their hair. I never saw a grey- or white-haired woman (other than the older 'sworn virgins') in Albania. Even in their traumatic situation, amongst Kosovar refugees, on occasions where older, even very old, women are not wearing headscarves, it could be observed that their hair is dyed. In cultures where the adaptation of 'male' clothing for women has become widely accepted, and grey hair considered normal for older women, this visual classification of the 'sworn virgin' might not be so convincing. However, in every description given of the 'sworn virgins', there is the added socio-cultural confirmation of this cross-gender transformation visible in their acquisition of non-biological body discipline: their masculine stance, mannerisms and actions. (This is also the case with the transgendered individuals of Cebuan society in the Phillipines: 'identification of ... (them) ... is based on both physical features and behavioural characteristics. However, cross-dressing is not essential for such classification.'[5])

Image and Identity

My interpreter Leonora was seen by some of the 'sworn virgins' to be in a similar situation to themselves. Like myself, she fitted the category of 'guest' and was treated as such, but as a native Albanian her role was also observed from their own view as a male one. Arta Dervishi also acted as an interpreter for her American anthropologist husband. She records her own study of the villages of Radomire in north-east Albania and confirms the continued existence of traditional life there in 1996, especially as it harshly affects women, in accordance with the *Kanun*. She discusses the confusion of her own identity: to the villagers she is primarily a wife, whose capacity as trans-lator allows her a heightened status. As a woman, Dervishi has access to information not available to her husband. Her urban upbringing in Tirana adds yet another dimension.[6]

Fashion and Function of Dress

Publications on fashion through the ages show distinctions between male and female garments. Men's wear has usually allowed for ease of movement while women's has tended to serve a more decorative function, especially wedding garb, which can be extremely ornate, heavy and restrictive. In traditional societies, women's apparel is often designed to display the wealth of her family (be it that of her father or that of her husband).

At times when men have worn a short skirt (for example Scottish kilts, Greek and Albanian fustanellas, Tudor tunics), women's clothes have often been contrastingly long thus still defining what apparel is seen as suitable for men and what for women.

Andromaqi Gjergji, the authority on Albanian dress, has written extensively on its rich variety. She notes that, 'dressing remains one of the most powerful manifestations of popular culture,'[7] and she distinguishes four functions of costume: practical, aesthetic, ceremonial and ritual.[8]

Traditionally it has been of importance to be dressed in fine clothes for burial. Grémaux heard reports that in the case of Mikas, one of the 'virgins' whom he discusses, in anticipation of her death, arranged for the purchase of a new set of clothing consisting of socks, woollen trousers, a vest and a cap in order to be suitably attired on her last journey. With the approval of the Orthodox priest, she was buried as a man in the Zabljak churchyard.[9] Grémaux heard similar reports of Tonë's funeral garb, who following her wishes was buried 'in the antiquated male costume she used to wear on special occasions', a photograph of her taken some years earlier was placed on the coffin.[10]

The differences in clothing between the sexes, age, marital status and locality (whether rural or urban)[11] strongly dictate the way people dress, especially the women. For example newly married women may wear bridal clothes for social events for a decade after their wedding.[12] Once married, rural women in particular are expected to conform by wearing headscarves. As in other areas of the Balkans these traditional expectations are changing.[13]

During the Communist era, it was demanded of foreign visitors that they also adhered to the strictly gendered dress code enforced on the Albanians: women were not permitted to wear mini-skirts or tight jeans. Men were to be clean shaven and were not to have long hair. Donert notes that 'Kadare highlights the absurdity of a country which allows hair to become a battlefield for young Albanian men to confront the state' and that 'the "politics of hair" demonstrates the relative unsophistication of Hoxha's attempts to control daily practise'.[14] It was assumed that people would be distracted from the building of socialism if they were allowed to become interested in such decadence as fashion.

However, by the 1970s, economic advantages began to be apparent in Albania as the new hydro-electric plants and factories built with Russian and Chinese assistance produced electricity and goods (though much of this was exported). During this period the textile industry blossomed, providing a wide variety of bright cloth which livened up summer apparel especially of the women who made their own clothes. Berit Backer commented that at this time 'the Albanian deal is a kind of traditional French style ... more European than East-European. To an occasional Western observer, an Albanian, when dressed up – looks more up-to-date than his Slavic brothers and sisters further East.'[15] During the Communist era, although there were barber's shops in every small town, there were no hairdressers for women. Any assistance needed would be provided within the family. The first hairdressing salons for women opened in the early 1990s.

Albanian Folk Dress

Gjergji notes that several traditional folk costumes relate to the most ancient cultures of the Balkans. She cites documents as evidence that some of them preserve a series of original features inherited from 'an ancient Illyrian sub-stratum'. Kadare emphasizes this perspective: 'Their dress was identical to the descriptions ... in ancient epic poetry ... they have not changed a thing in a thousand years. Their black cloaks had shoulder-pads decorated with truncated or atrophied winglets that made you shiver. Looking on these highlanders, you were looking at the boundary between men and gods.'[16]

Immediately neighbouring Albania, and sharing the barren range known as *Bjeshkët e Namuna* (the Accursed Mountains), Montenegro maintained legal independence through five centuries of Ottoman domination. Barbara Denich states that its 'heroic tradition is ... expressed in the national costume of these regions, in which men are splendid figures with midriffs bedecked in long sashes and assorted weaponry'.[17]

Gjergji draws attention to the fact that Albanian dress has attracted foreign artists and writers over several centuries. She cites the example of Spenser, the Elizabethan playwright, who dressed some of the characters of his *Faerie Queen* in 'the Albanian fashion'.[18] She also observes that the Albanian rejection of the Oriental influence on attire in the late eighteenth and through-out the nineteenth century served as 'a clearcut political aspect and this is attributed, without doubt to the major efforts of our men of National Renaissance to preserve the purity of our national language and culture'.[19] Many foreigners have been inspired by Albanian dress.[20] Ferid Hudhri has collected together copies of artwork of well-known foreign artists in his book *Albania and Albanians in World Art*.[21] The wide variety of apparel portrayed is due in large part to the fact that the artists were working over a period of hundreds of years and in areas which at those times were even less easily accessible to one another than they are now. Corot's portrait of a young Albanian woman has been exhibited all over the world. She wears a low-necked, white, embroidered blouse with a red *jelek* (traditional waistcoat) and gold ornamentation. Her dark hair flows from beneath a headscarf of red and gold, matching her *jelek*. She is wearing dangling gold earrings, though no bracelets are visible in the painting.[22]

Aprons and Veils: Women's Dress in Albania

In drawing from the literature on the wealth and variety of Albanian clothing, by region, religion, sex and historical period, I have chosen to concentrate specifically on two garments: veils and traditional embroidered aprons. These garments are both often considered to belong to underdeveloped societies, discarded by women in modern industrial occupations. Neither would ever be worn by 'sworn virgins'. These two garments may be seen to symbolize the covering of seductive and reproductive parts of the female body (mouth, hair and genitals). Aprons have lost any such conscious purpose and, along with headscarves and skirts, are the most obviously visible universal female attire in the regions under consideration. Tone Bringa elaborates on the symbolically varying ways of tying a headscarf;[23] she also notes that 'When secular symbols through which the difference has been expressed disappear, new ones take their place.'[24]

Unlike the richly hand-decorated aprons described by Gjergji, those which are worn generally are very simple and functional. In the photograph on p. we see a woman wearing the dress of the Has region – quite similar to that known as Rrafsh Dukagjini (the Field of Duke John) originating in Western Kosov@. It consists of a knee-length cotton shirt worn with a vest and *two* woollen aprons, a big one at the front (the *përparja*) and a small one (in Kosov@ called the *prapa*, meaning back) to sit on, to prevent the shirt from getting dirty.[25] In her article on aprons in Albanian popular dress, Gjergji suggests that apron types worn by rural women until very recently reflected the social and marital status of the wearer, her age, religion and the occasion on which the items of clothing were worn, along with regional and local variations according to fabric, shape, location and use.[26] She makes the case for clothing that, 'though at first it had only a protective function, it soon acquired magical, aesthetic and other functions'.[27]

Gjergji traces the development of dress, and specifically aprons, as a visual representation of changing values and influences. For example, a certain apron type existed in Labëria before the Eastern influence of Islam introduced *dimi* (or *dimite*) (Eastern baggy trousers).[28] With the introduction of these trousers in other regions, the functional apron was tucked in or removed, and the festive apron became reduced to 'little more than a decorative belt'.[29] Similarly, of the trapeze-shaped aprons worn by Orthodox women in some parts of southern Albania, Gjergji writes: 'I believe these aprons show the influence of urban culture on the rural bridal costume in the last decades of the nineteenth century.'[30] One variant of this apron type apparently originated only at the end of the last century, appearing first in the clothes of urban women, indicating an imitation of Western fashion. These coexisted with the more traditional apron considered essential to female festive dress.[31] The urban influence is so strong that in some cases it even came to transcend religious discrepancies: 'a number of family photographs of the period show such aprons . . . worn thenceforth not only by Orthodox women but also by Moslem women, the urban costume beginning to become more uniform'.[32] Gjergji explains the absence of aprons from monuments of the antique period by contrasting the very different dress style of the Illyrian women who were represented in these high forms of art in which rural women simply did not feature.[33]

Veils clearly denote the religion of the wearer. It may be of significance that I met no veiled women amongst members of the households that I visited.

In contrast to the more generally accepted argument for the veil as a symbol of imprisonment, Reineck's and El Guindi's theories of invulnerability/ anonymity have been included in this chapter to demonstrate the importance of the veil as a feature of dress. The 'feeling of nakedness' (shame, as discussed in chapter 2), described by some Muslim women after their veils were removed, must be seen in its anthropological context. To these women, the veil constitutes an extremely important part of the idea of 'getting dressed', whereas in the West the veil represents a symbol of male dominance and the social control of women.

In Albania, as a predominantly Muslim country, the veil was commonly worn well into the twentieth century. It was discouraged under Zog in the 1920s and 1930s, and under Communism forbidden, as it signified adherence to religion. By 1967 when Albania was declared an atheist state, it is likely that few dared to wear a veil. Since 1990 there has been a rebirth of religion including the following of Islam and the return of the veil for some of its believers, in particular young women. However, many Albanian women consider this a retrograde development. In Kosov@, where Yugoslavia's atheism was less rigidly enforced, the veil continued to be worn by some women. Reineck offers a rather unusual opinion on the function of the veil, commenting that 'Contrary to the Western notion that veiling imprisons women, some Albanians who have worn a veil say it creates a kind of freedom by giving them anonymity and symbolic invulnerability when outside the

Figure 29. Village bride. Her magnificent bridal attire consists of a red woollen headscarf, a white cotton blouse whose long sleeves are decorated with red and yellow embroidered flowers; the lavish collar is likewise decorated. Her pleated white skirt is made from Albanian cotton, under which she wears woollen trousers held up with elastic. Round her waist, the bride wears a broad cotton belt of yellow and black, with long red, yellow, white and blue tassels. She wears two waistcoats, a tight-fitting one of red and blue silk with golden edging, and over it a black woollen one hanging loosly. In her lace-gloved hands the bride holds a cotton embroidered kerchief; her shoes are simple, black and low-heeled. Ann Christine Eek (Samfoto, Norway), outside Kukës, 1994

home.' Kikrije, a woman she interviewed, told her, 'Without it we felt naked. They offered us money to take it off, but we refused. When we finally took it off the men made us stay home. I remember the first time I went out without it – I couldn't stop crying. For a year we went out only at night.'[34] Fadwa El Guindi's book *Veil: Modesty, Privacy and Resistance* is devoted to exactly the question of the experience of liberation through the wearing of the veil. Her book describes a return to the veil and comments on its popularity since the 1990s as a demarginalization of women in society: she suggests that the veil provides a symbol of resistance especially where it provides a liberation from colonial legacies.[35] Reineck also found that:

> Young brides boast about the extent to which they have been sheltered by natal families and in-laws as a sign of their worth … proud of their untarnished reputations and their respect for tradition … Separation from men during social gatherings also gives them a sense of freedom. Due to the strict rules of propriety and shame associated with mixed groups, when women are alone they are infinitely freer to express themselves, to relax, to have a good time … social contact between men and women tends to be sexually loaded … Thus while Western women tend to see segregation and seclusion as 'keeping women in', to Kosova women it usually means 'keeping men out'.[36]

Trousers and 'Skull Caps': Traditional Male Dress

Edith Durham sketched and painted many people in regional dress and painstakingly portrayed detailed traditional variations especially in the embroidery of cuffs and collars. Many of her paintings and drawings depicted men wearing *potur*, the traditional trousers of northern Albania, low-slung garments of white homespun wool, with black braid sewn vertically down the outside of each leg.[37] These have been romantically described by Kadare 'trousers, the colour of milk, with a dotted black zigzag line down the side, roughly the shape of the symbol for high-voltage electricity'.[38]

Men in traditional attire also feature predominantly in many of Edward Lear's magnificent landscapes depicting scenes from all over Albania. He managed to capture the changes in pattern, fabric and style of dress, depending on locality. For example he painted a market scene outside Berat (south central Albania) in which the men's clothing is predominantly white, though the men still wear skirts and their headgear consists of red fezes with black tassles. Contrastingly, in his lithograph of 'Shkodër 1848' (in northern Albania) painted the same year, several men in black cloaks are seen interacting beside the lake, some seated, some standing. Men in Suliot dress: white turbans, white cloaks lined with dark material, elaborate waistbands with intricate

Figure 30. Sokol in 'skull cap', with nephew. AY: outside Bajram Curri, 1996

embroidery, also feature in Delacroix's paintings.[39] They are portrayed wearing white fustanellas and shirts showing beneath their flowing black cloaks and on their heads white *qeleshe* ('skull caps').[40]

The term 'skull cap', so-called in English, describes how these white woollen felt caps closely hug the wearer's head. Contrary to common speculation, they do not indicate Izlamicization, and are worn also by Christians. They are never worn by women and they are more commonly seen on the heads of older men, from the villages rather than from the towns. They are often worn within the home. Being typical male attire, these caps are a 'marquer' of their masculinity. Two of the 'sworn virgins' I personally met donned such headgear.

A recent and tragic example of the mythologization of the symbol of the traditional white 'skull cap' is evident in this excerpt of news on the ethnic cleansing of Kosov@: 'In many places the Serbs compounded the fear with humiliation. Older men were beaten for wearing the white conical hats of the Albanian mountains or forced to make the Serbian Orthodox three-fingered sign. One refugee convoy passed row on row of white conical hats set atop fence posts.'[41] Even though the white 'skull cap' is not of religious significance in Albania, it has been taken as a symbol of religious as well as ethnic affiliation in Kosov@ – perhaps because Kosovars adhere more strictly to the Muslim religion than their counterparts in Albania.

A photograph published on the front cover of the *Guardian Editor*,[42] shows a young Kosovar Albanian carrying an elderly man in a convoy of refugees – fear and sadness in their eyes. The hats they wear represent the generational gap: the younger man wears a flat cap, the older man wears a 'skull cap'. A contrast can also be seen in the caps of rural 'sworn virgins'.

Children and Dress

Children are considered to be a gender-neutral group, as expressed by the languages of many cultures (e.g. German for child, *kind*, and Serbo-Croatian *dete*, both conjugate as neuter nouns). In some cultures we assume that the colour of baby clothes has always been gender-specific. However, it is important to note that 'only after World War II, the *Times* reported, did the present alignment of the two genders with pink and blue come into being.'[43]

Gjergji cites ages up to nine as being those during which children in Albania are all dressed similarly. From the time of his first haircut, a boy thus gendered is vulnerable as a potential bloodfeud victim. For this reason the first haircut was often delayed for several years. From around age twelve, boys in Albania traditionally were dressed in a masculine way 'whereas the girls of that same age were considered grown-ups and should dress as simply as possible, and especially be careful to hide their hair by the headdress tied under the chin around the neck.' It is for the protection of family honour that girls, especially from the age of puberty, are expected to dress modestly. This is also the time when girls begin to wear veils if they are to conform to strict Muslim mores.

Cross-Dressing in the Balkans

Ismail Kadare has collected together into a magnificent visual study, some of the thousands of studio portraits of Albanians at the turn of the nineteenth century. Through the Marubi Studio in Shkodër, photography was first introduced into northern Albania in 1864. Kadare's selection includes a plate showing 'Homme vetu d'un costume de femme catholique' (A man dressed in the costume of a Catholic woman). No further explanation is given for this unusual cross-dressing, certainly a curiosity in an area of the world most known for its extreme patriarchy (see Figure 31).[44]

'Sworn virgins' in the Balkans on the contrary, usually dress in men's attire, formerly in traditional clothing (see Figure 1, and for a modification of this, see photo of Dilore, Figure 22). It consisted of tightly fitting white felt trousers (*potur*) and jacket (*mitan*) with black braid trimming, 'a skull cap' also made

Figure 31. A man dressed in Catholic women's clothing (early 20th century). A photograph in the Marubi Studio archive, Shkodër; also in Ismail Kadare's collection of Marubi photographs (Kadare (1995), *Albania: visage des Balkans. Ecrits de lumière* (Albania: Face of the Balkans. Writing with Light)). Kel Marubi, Skhodër studio, between 1900 and 1919

of white felt, and for footwear *opanke* (a type of enclosed leather sandal). Although Gjergji comments that 'sworn virgins' wear 'partly . . . men's clothes, partly . . . women's clothes', but does not clarify the exact women's garments which were worn, all the 'sworn virgins' whom I met dressed entirely in men's outer clothing, whether traditional or Western and all used strictly masculine body discipline in stature, walk and actions. They all appeared completely comfortable with their self-image (apart from Medi on our first meeting only).

Variation in clothing among the 'sworn virgins' I met, reflects their occupation and status, for example, Dilore's traditional wear as a revered village elder contrasts to that of Sanie's denim shirt and jeans of a truck-driver. Those in the towns more frequently wear suits, which rural men (and 'sworn virgins') keep for special occasions. Rougher attire is usually worn by farmers. Footwear is also an indicator of gender: Medi was an exception, with her trainers (which have not been generally adopted by women in Albania). All the other 'sworn virgins' I met had heavy boots or shoes. Albanian women wear lighter shoes which may be slip-ons or, in the towns, high-heeled. I never met a 'sworn virgin' wearing a skirt.

The greatest visual variation I found, however, was in physical development which made it apparent that while almost all 'sworn virgins' were completely flat-chested, two of them wore upper undergarments usually reserved for women. For formal occasions, especially weddings, men traditionally wear a *xhamadan* (embroidered ceremonial marriage waistcoat). Dilore specifically commented that she wore this as 'headman' in the *dashmor* (custom of fetching a bride to her wedding). With the gradual transition to Western-style clothing, it seems that most 'sworn virgins' now wear Western men's wear. Deborah Gannett reports of a nineteenth-century cross-dresser: 'wearing breeches entitled her to a freedom she had never before experienced: "a new world now opened to my view, the objects of which seemed as important as the transition before seemed unnatural"'.[45] Certainly by wearing male apparel the self-image of the 'virgins' is confirmed. Pashke (see p. 77) aptly clarified that 'to dress as a man earns the respect due to a man'.

Notes

1. Gjergji, A. (1988), *Veshjet Shqiptare në Shekuj: Origjina Tipologjia Zhvillimi* (Albanian Costume Through the Centuries: Origin, Typology, Development), Tirana: Academy of Sciences, p. 236. In this very comprehensive volume, Gjergji even gives detailed patterns which may be used to produce authentic garments.

2. Eicher, J.B. and Roach-Higgins, M.E. (1992), *Dress and Gender: Making and Meaning in Cultural Contexts*, New York; Oxford: St Martin's Press, p. 12.

3. Joanne B. Eicher and Mary Ellen Roach-Higgins have devoted a whole chapter to this subject, with some crucial conclusions. Eicher and Roach-Higgins (1992), *Dress and Gender*, chapter 1, pp. 8–28.

4. Goffman, E. (1959), *The Presentation of Self in Everyday Life*, Garden City, New York: Doubleday Anchor Books, p. 25.

5. Herdt, G. (ed.) (1994), *Third Sex, Third Gender: Beyond Sexual Dimorphism in Culture and History*, New York: Zone Books, p. 45.

6. Dervishi, A. (1996), *Tales from the Wilderness: the Making of an Albanian Feminist Anthropologist*, MA thesis, University of Texas at Austin.

7. Gjergji (1988), *Veshjet Shqiptare në Shekuj*, p. 233.

8. Gjergji, A. (1994), 'Variations in Traditional Clothing According to its Function', *Zeitschrift für Balkanologie*, vol. 30, no. 2, pp. 131–48.

9. Grémaux, R. (1994), 'Woman Becomes Man in the Balkans' in Herdt, G. (ed.), *Third Sex, Third Gender: Beyond Sexual Dimorphism in Culture and History*, New York: Zone Books, p. 253.

10. Grémaux (1989), 'Mannish Women of the Balkan Mountains', in Bremmer, J. (ed.), from Sappho to de Sade: Moments in the History of Sexuality, London: Routledge, p. 152.

11. Bringa makes this point: Bringa, T. (1995), *Being Muslim the Bosnian Way: Identity and Community in a Central Bosnian Village*, Princeton, New Jersey: Princeton University Press, p. 62.

12. Reineck, J. (1991), *The Past as Refuge: Gender, Migration and Ideology among the Kosova Albanians*, Ph. D. thesis, University of California at Berkeley, p. 99.

13. See Bringa (1995), *Being Muslim the Bosnian Way*, pp. 102 and 118.

14. Donert, C. (1999), *Trees of Blood and Trees of Milk: Customary Law and the Construction of Gender in Albania*, MA thesis, Albanian Studies, School for Slavonic and East European Studies, University of London, pp. 10–11

15. Backer, B. Unpublished manuscript, written 1981–5.

16. Kadare, I. (1997), *The File on H*, translated by David Bellow from the French version of the Albanian by Jusuf Vrioni, London: The Harvill Press, p. 73.

17. Denich, B.S. (1974), 'Sex and Power in the Balkans' in Rosaldo, M.Z. and Lamphere, L. (eds), *Woman, Culture and Society*, Stanford, California: Stanford University Press, p. 247.

18. Rabelais mentioned a 'chapeau albanois' in his *Gargantua et Pantagruel*.

19. Gjergji (1988), *Veshjet Shqiptare në Shekuj*, p. 244.

20. See the painting by Thomas Phillips (1814), 'George Gordon, Lord Byron in Suliot costume' in the National Portrait Gallery, London; and the photograph of Edith Durham in Allcock, J. B. and Young, A. (eds) (1991), *Black Lambs and Grey Falcons: Women Travellers in the Balkans*, Bradford: Bradford University Press, following p. 89. Republication (forthcoming 2000), Oxford; New York: Berghahn.

21. Hudhri, F. (1990), *Albania and the Albanians in World Art*, Athens: Christos Giovanis A.E.B.E. Amongst the artists included are Barret, Beresford, Bellini Bianchini, Cartwright, Çermak, Cockerell, Corot, De-camps, Delacroix, Durham, Jerome, Gleyre, Irton, Lear, Lipparini, Magaud, Oprandi, Philips, Sargent, Von Stakelberg, Valerio, Woodville.

22. Hudhri (1990), *Albania and Albanians in World Art*, p. 133.

23. Bringa (1995), *Being Muslim the Bosnian Way*, pp. 62–3.

24. Bringa (1995), *Being Muslim the Bosnian Way*, p. 80.

25. Gjergji (1986), *Veshjet Shqiptare në Shekuj*, p. 140.

26. Gjergji, A. (1986), 'Aprons in Albanian Popular Costume', *Costume*, no. 20, pp. 44–62.

27. Gjergji (1986), 'Aprons in Albanian Popular Costume', p. 44.

28. Gjergji (1986), 'Aprons in Albanian Popular Costume', p. 51. See also Bringa's

comments on the introduction of Turkish fashion under Ottoman domination: Bringa (1995), *Being Muslim the Bosnian Way*, f. 16, p. 240.

29. Gjergji (1986), 'Aprons in Albanian Popular Costume', p. 56.

30. Gjergji (1986), 'Aprons in Albanian Popular Costume', p. 53.

31. Gjergji (1986), 'Aprons in Albanian Popular Costume', p. 55.

32. Gjergji (1986), 'Aprons in Albanian Popular Costume', p. 55.

33. Gjergji (1986), 'Aprons in Albanian Popular Costume', p. 61.

34. Reineck (1991), *The Past as Refuge*, p. 104.

35. El Guindi, F. (forthcoming), *Veil: Modesty, Privacy and Resistance*, Oxford, UK; New York: Berg Publishers.

36. Reineck (1991), *The Past as Refuge*, p. 105. Reineck here draws on the writing of Backer, B. (1979), *Behind the Stone Walls: Changing Household Organization among the Albanians of Kosovo*, Oslo: PRIO publications S-8/79; Dwyer, D.H. (1978), *Images and Self-Images: Male and Female in Morocco*, New York: Columbia University Press; and Nelson, C. (1974), 'Public and Private Politics: Women in the Middle Eastern World', *American Ethnologist*, vol. 1, no. 3.

37. Hudhri (1990), *Albania and Albanians in World Art*, p. 196. See also her careful drawings in Start, L.E. (1977), with notes by Edith Durham, *The Durham Collection of Garments and Embroideries from Albania and Yugoslavia*, Halifax: Calderdale Museums (Bankfield Museum Notes, Series, no. 4, plate 16).

38. Kadare (1997), *The File on H*, p. 73.

39. Hudhri (1990), *Albania and Albanians in World Art*, for example see pp. 131, 158–61.

40. Hudhri (1990), *Albania and Albanians in World Art*, p. 145.

41. Reported on internet, ALBANEWS, 27 May 1999.

42. Front cover photography of *Guardian Editor*, 10 April 1999.

43. Garber, M. (1992), *Vested Interests: Cross-Dressing and Cultural Anxiety*, New York; London: Routledge, p. 236.

44. Kadare, I. (1995), *Albanie: Visage des Balkans. Ecrits de Lumière* (Albania: Face of the Balkans. Writing with Light), Photographs by Marubi, P., K. and G.; text translated from the Albanian by Vrioni, J. and Zbynovsky, E., Paris: Arthaud, plate 26. On enquiry, Kadare could offer no explanation. Others have suggested this was carnival attire.

45. Gannett, D. (1802), *An Address Delivered with Applause, At the Federal-Street Theatre, Boston, 4 Succesive Nights of the Different Plays, beginning March 22, 1802*, published at the request of the audience, Dedham, 1802, p. 6, quoted in Wheelwright (1990), *Amazons and Military Maids*, p. 133.

7

Asserting their Masculinity: Men and 'Sworn Virgins'

Gender is social practise that constantly refers to bodies and what bodies do, it is not social practise reduced to the body. Indeed reductionism presents the exact reverse of the real situation. Gender exists precisely to the extent that biology does *not* determine the social. It marks one of those points of transition where historical process supersedes biological evolution as the form of change. Gender is a scandal, an outrage, from the point of view of essentialism. Sociobiologists are constantly trying to abolish it, by proving that human social arrangements are a reflex of evolutionary imperatives.

R.W. Connell, *Masculinities*[1]

Female-to-male Cross-Dressers

Through the ages, and in different parts of the world, there have been widely varying attitudes to cross-dressing. It is only during the twentieth century that discussion of lesbianism has evolved, through such acclaimed figures as Virginia Woolf. There is no reference to it in Shakespeare although many of his plays involved cross-dressing, a subject which has inspired a broad literature, leading to such erudite statements as that of Camile Paglia of Viola in *Twelfth Night*. Paglia points out that Viola is in an 'ambiguous role as a go-between . . . conveying Orsino's masochistic endearments to the arrogant Olivia'. Paglia concludes therefore that Viola is 'an androgyne bearing a hermaphroditic message from one androgyne to another'.[2]

Today we tend only to look back as far as the 1920s as the time when fashion attempted to bring a similarity to the clothes of both sexes. At that time of the emancipation of women in the Western world, a boyish look for women became fashionable. Flat-chested women with short hair, sometimes wearing trousers and a tie reflected the changing age. However, as Julie Wheelwright notes, even in seventeenth-century London it was common for actresses to don male clothing.[3] 'By satirizing or mocking deviants, the drama defined norms and by the eighteenth century the female warrior had become a popular, even conventional, heroine.'[4] The same might be said of the

Japanese *Takarazuka*, the popular revue company which employs only females aged 15–18 to play male parts in their musicals.[5] During the nineteenth century there were music-halls and other places of entertainment in London where women could rent male attire at the door. However, with the changing mores of Victorian Britain 'a dramatic rewriting of history subsequently took place ... the female soldiers and sailors were erased from the record or reduced to the occasional footnote. The female soldiers who were hailed as heroines, albeit exceptions a century earlier, became portrayed as amusing freaks of nature and their stories examples of "coarseness and triviality".'[6]

Wheelwright warns against interpreting the acts of these women as 'an intentional and self-conscious desire to defy the prevailing notions of sexual difference'[7] and notes that 'Cross-dressing for women often remained a process of imitation rather than a self-conscious claim by women for the social privileges given exclusively to men. Their exploits challenged existing categories of sexual difference but the terms of the debate usually remained the same.'[8] Her book studies the individual stories of many women who for varying reasons chose to take the role of men, in most cases in order to gain positions which they perceived to be advantageous, many in the military, which were not open to women. Some of the stories tell of women going to war in order to pursue a loved one (a theme particularly popular in ballad form). Many saw their entrance into the man's world as an escape from powerlessness, drudgery and boredom in strict Victorian society; others saw it as a way out of an unsatisfactory marriage; some were lesbians 'who bravely risked ostracism and punishment by symbolically claiming the right to women's erotic love through their assumption of male clothing'.[9] According to Devor, many were not lesbians, but were categorized thus out of a lack of the terminology to describe them at that time: 'In the new parlance, female partial crossdressers, who had previously been known as "inverts" for their abandonment of their socially appropriate gender roles, came to be commonly thought of as "lesbians". For most of the twentieth century, the term *lesbian* was closely associated with "mannish women".'[10]

Many accounts portray women acting individually rather than for any cause, feminist or other, and unconcerned about changing society themselves. Many of the escapees show disdain for other women, preferring the roughness and camaraderie of men's company, especially on equal terms. Clearly war offered opportunities which at other times were harder to find; it gave them an identity and an acceptable patriotic motive for leaving home. Flora Sandes, who served in the Serbian Army,[11] found difficult contradiction when attending functions as a woman amongst those who treated her as a man.[12] Likewise she and others were uneasy with their roles when the war was over and they reverted to their feminine identities.[13]

There are also Albanian cross-dressers who became heroines and warriors. Shote Galica, the well-known Albanian woman dressed as a soldier and accompanied her husband in the forces fighting against invading Serbs in 1924.[14] Galica's heroism is recognized as an effort to defend her country. She outlived her husband, and continued to fight after his death. No Albanian would consider Galica a 'sworn virgin', for the primary role of such a person is as a family head rather than as a fighter. Once the fighting was over, Shote took her place as a widow probably in appropriate women's black attire, albeit a highly praised widow. Likewise in the seventeenth century Nora of Kelmendi, (also known as *Nora e Bukur*, Nora the Beautiful) who probably dressed as a man, was equally renowned for her resistance to invading Ottoman Turks. Legend has it that the ruling Pasha agreed to leave the area on condition that Nora was handed over to him. She slayed the Pasha, thus sacrificing herself for the sake of her own honour and her country's freedom. Her bravery was recognized by the Turks who executed her as a man.

Where 'sworn virgins' differ significantly from many of the cross-dressers referred to above is that they are taking on a lifelong change. Furthermore this change is in no way seen as deviant within their society; it is not the result of some psychological or physiological difference, but as a status within an orderly pattern of statuses. It was certainly my experience in all my interactions with 'sworn virgins' and those acquainted in any way with them that, as Backer points out 'there is no suspicion of any "sexual deviance" thrown upon these females, as everybody seems to recognize the phenomenon as a purely social choice between different life styles'.[15] The accepted status is marked in a logical and regular fashion by the adoption of appropriate dress. To become a 'sworn virgin' is a dramatic illustration of the sociological concept of 'putting on a role', rather than an occasion on which some inner self is permitted to 'come out', by pushing aside certain socio-cultural conventions.

Transsexuals and Cross-Dressers in Other Cultures

Holly Devor asserts that there have probably always been female-to-male transsexuals.[16] Many studies have been made of various Native American groups, and the term *berdache* has long been understood to cover a range of Native American gender types, roles and behaviours. Much has been written on the subject, not least Walter Williams' *The Spirit and the Flesh*.[17] Sue-Ellen Jacobs and Wesley Thomas recently claimed, however, that the term *berdache* is derogatory given its origin. They explain the origin 'derives from sixteenth century Persian by way of French and literally means "catamite" or "boy kept for unnatural purposes"'. Instead, the authors tell us, we should use 'two-spirit' as a term 'created by the community that it designates and defines'.[18] This is an all-encompassing generic term describing any kind of non-heterosexual relationship: gay, lesbian, transgendered (cross-dressers, transvestites and transsexuals).

There are many parallels to be drawn and comparisons to be made with the Albanian 'sworn virgins' and transsexuals and cross-dressers in other parts of the world. 'Dress', as defined in Chapter 6, clearly contributes considerably to the construction of gender in all of these cases.

Peter Phillimore has studied the situation of the *sadhin* (the feminine form of *sadhu* or holy man) – the term given to a small number of celibate Hindu women living in Himachal Pradesh, India. Like the 'sworn virgins' of the Balkans, they dress as men and practise lifelong secular celibacy, although unlike the 'sworn virgins' they take no vows.[19] Another feature that the phenomena have in common is that lifelong chastity is recognized as an alternative to marriage, especially where there is a lack of brothers. Also like the 'virgins' 'theirs is a wholly respectable status'.[20] Phillimore finds that the practise draws on a repertoire of symbols familiar from Hindu and neighbouring Buddhist renunciatory traditions. A *sadhin* lives in cultural denial of her sexual identity, adopting her status, usually by her own choice, before puberty, suggesting connections with a wider tradition of renunciation and asceticism. Philimore explores the tensions and ambiguities which arise from 'the construct of lifelong secular celibacy in a cultural setting which ordinarily recognizes no such possibility for women'.[21] The crux of Philimore's argument concerns the ambiguity surrounding the degree to which their status is locally construed as sacred versus secular, not that concerning their gender. He remains convinced that no 'gender switch' takes place, and that their dress represents only a 'female rendering of men's clothing'.

Abigail Haworth relates that in the South Pacific islands of Samoa, as many as one family in five has a son who lives as a woman.[22] Brought up from an early age with a female identity, these young men wear flowers in their hair and dress as girls. The institution is known as *fa'afafine*, literally 'a male who is like a female' and is seen as a necessary adjustment for the proportions of women needed in their balanced society. Haworth learned from interviews that these 'women' find sexual partners amongst young men of their villages 'never other *fa'afafine*. "That would be lesbianism" exclaims Mishie, one *fa'afafine*, with horror. "We only go with straight men, and we always take the passive role in sex".' However, their inability to bear children makes them less desirable long-term partners and Mishie admits to being lonely at times. According to the folklore of Polynesian culture, one of the male siblings in a family was often raised as a *fa'afafine* if there were not enough biological females to deal with domestic chores. 'The child was dressed like a girl and was expected to behave like one – that is, to cook and clean, play nursemaid to elderly relatives and generally add an extra touch of "feminine" warmth to the family. When he grew up the *fa'afafine* would not marry but devote himself to caring for his elderly parents.'[23] Haworth quotes one *fa'afafine* as saying 'they feel this is the one child who won't desert them'. Because this kind of gender transferral is socially acceptable in Samoan society 'a boy ... from an early age grows up as a girl with the support and often encouragement of his family'. Haworth makes the case that the tradition has been passed down through generations of young boys emulating older *fa'afafine*, 'or simply wanting to act and dress like a woman in a social climate where such behaviour carries no taboo'.[24] Their function in society is seen to serve a very constructive role.

Early missionaries were not able to influence the *fa'afafine* to wear male attire but 'were so successful at converting the population to Christianity that rather ironically, many of the sopranos in church choirs are *fa'afafine*'.[25]

However, in contrast to the 'sworn virgins' in the Balkans, their high level of acceptance does not prevent discrimination against them in the same way women are discriminated against: 'the *fa'afafine* are, by definition "like a female" and therefore must share the same low status as women in Samoan society and like women, *fa'afafine* are expected to be chaste.'[26]

In a rapidly changing world, and one in which there is far greater contact between cultures than ever before, there are fears for the future of these transgendered individuals. These days, like many Samoans, some *fa'afafine* want to go abroad to work. But there is the worry that they may encounter rejection and face the kind of long-term psychological problems associated with it. Brownie Tuiasopo, a village chief, worries for his teenage *fa'afafine* son. 'I don't want him to be tied to Samoa. But where else would they treat a young man who wears dresses, who walks and talks like a woman, as if he was a normal member of society?'[27] Rejection based on misunderstandings arising from culturally constructed gender stereotypes, could have far-reaching psychological implications for the *fa'afafine*. Similar problems could also be experienced by 'sworn virgins' who go abroad or even to the capital to work. It is easy to see how a very real identity crisis could result from the attempt to be integrated into a society which might treat these women as women (their masculine attire elsewhere not indicative of masculine gender) when they had grown up expecting to be treated as men.

Joel Halpern draws attention to a similar option for men to be women in Laos; they however have the possibility to revert back to the gender of their birth.[28]

Another culture, where certain specified persons change gender has been studied by John Wood. In East Africa, the Gabra are camel-herding nomads of Kenya's northern and Ethiopia's southern deserts. They are from areas where water (in the south) and pasture (in the north) are each available seasonally, but at considerable distances from one another and the rare rainfalls are torrential. The total number of Gabra is around 35,000. They live in mobile groups of up to sixty persons and are:

> ... as masculine and virile and patriarchal as men come. They carry knives and spears and nowadays even machine guns to protect their herds. They prize vigor and toughness, the capacity to walk long distances without food or water. A man who has killed an enemy and returned with his severed genitals is honored above others. Men say that women are *nus* (half); they say women are children. They exclude women from political and ritual activities. They denigrate women and feminine things. Yet they regard their most prestigious men as women.[29]

Wood suggests that the sort of gender ambiguity found amongst the Gabra prompts questions about 'what it means for a man to be a woman, and what, if not sex, organizes gender assignments'.[30] He uses his findings with this group of West Africans to develop a theory of gender as a spatial as much as a sexual construction. He discusses 'inside-outside' or 'center-periphery' as both metaphorical and physical concepts in reaching an under-standing of the place of these men-who-become-women. During most of the year the women move their camps about once each month, while the men travel with their camel herds, hence the concepts of central and periphal. '... women characterize and define the social center and thereby also the moral center'.[31] Thus Wood suggests 'it is when men shift their attention from that masculine outside to the feminine inside that they become women.'

The men who earn the prestigious title of *d'abella* only achieve it in later life. From that time on they are treated as women but with special extra responsibilities to lead prayers and oversee ritual performances. Dress forms a very important part of this ritual. They wear plain white cloth and although they do not dress exactly as women, they tie their cloth on the left side of their body, like women. They are addressed as women and refer to themselves as women, they cease to carry or even to speak of weapons, and they urinate in a squatting position. According to the Gabra, the *d'abella* 'give birth' to culture.

Wood also, makes the point that although gender is a spatially constructed concept amongst the Gabra, it is actually dress which defines their gender roles: 'the bifurcation of space and its relation to gender is reflected in Gabra clothing, and the dynamics of dress illustrate the spatial argument ... Dress locates Gabra symbolically'.[32] Wood notes that with the influence of Western culture and urbanization, men visiting the cities will alter their manner of dress to conform with the conventions of modernity. Women, however, help maintain their Gabra tradition by not altering their customary attire: 'In the face of modernity, women rather than men mark ethnicity.'[33]

A Third Gender

As Wood claims in his book on the Gabra, one major flaw in Western discourse on transgenderism is that we find it very difficult to break away from the basic dichotomy of male-female in our analysis of gender. Even within the homosexual community we tend to see a breakdown according to traditional gender stereotypes, with one member of a partnership taking the 'active', the other the 'passive' role.[34]

Likewise in analysing the 'sworn virgins' of Albania, it becomes very difficult to break away from an attempt to categorize them as either 'male' or 'female'. Mildred Dickemann has called them 'transgendered individuals who have become social men leading masculine lives', enjoying the traditional status, role and identity of social men, the only such socially recognized transgendered status in modern Europe.[35]

Wood goes so far as to assert that decategorization and the development of a 'third gender' concept has thus far never been successfully attempted by anyone, with the possible exception of Herdt. 'Even the literature on so-called "third" genders describes alternative configurations of "masculine" and "feminine" characters, rather than some other third, fourth, or fifth characters.'[36] This dichotomy has obvious implications for dress.

Marjorie Garber cites the amusing analogy of the public restroom as a blatant modern symbol of the cultural binarism of gender: 'Cross-dressers who want to pass prefer to read the stick figures literally:

> those in pants, in there; those in skirts, in here. The public restroom appears repeatedly in transvestite accounts of passing in part because it so directly posits the binarism of gender (choose either one door or the other) in apparently inflexible terms, and also (what is part of the same point) because it marks a place of taboo.[37]

Interestingly, Wood himself actually works within the framework of the traditional bipolarity in which Western thought has typically packaged gender. He criticizes poststructuralist theories for their definition of binary as two, calling instead for a redefinition of the terminology: 'Binarity does not necessarily reduce gender hegemonically to "this" or "that." Rather the term refers to a distinction between "this" or "not this".'[38] Wood asserts that the Gabra themselves pose an answer to the difficult question of gender categorizaton in that their spatial binarity exists along a continuum which creates a fluidity that can allow gender to cross over anatomical lines: 'Gabra do not pose a third gender with *d'abella*, but reconfigure the masculine-feminine, disposed in both ways.'[39] Wood's ethnographic studies into the Gabra confirm how gender relates to sex, but is not necessarily reduced to it: 'In this case, binary structure does not in and of itself limit gender expressions, it expands them.'[40] In many ways, dress itself can become an expression of the multiplicity of gender issues.

According to Anne Bolin's 'five-form model of gender variance', the Navajo:

> recognize three physical sexes: hermaphrodites, males and females, and at least three or more gender statuses: men (boys), women (girls), and *nadle*. There are three kinds of *nadle*: real *nadle* and *nadle* pretenders who may be genital men (males) and women (females) . . . They assume occupational tasks and behaviors associated with women but they also have special rights not shared by other Navajo.[41]

Nadle sex partners may include women or men but not other *nadle* or *nadle* pretenders. Homosexuality defined as intercourse with partners of the same gender is not permitted (as with the *fa'afafine*, mentioned earlier in this chapter). Bolin explains that this illustrates problems in cross-cultural interpretation: 'If the *nadle* is a third gender status, then the term homosexual is meaningless and illustrates that Western concepts of sexual orientation and behavior are linked to the polarity of that of gender schema.'[42]

In her study 'Binary versus Multiple: Cultural Constructions of Sex and Gender', Sabine Lang argues that cultures differ widely in the ways they recognize and value ambiguity in terms of sex and gender, such as 'intersexed individuals' (those born with both male and female external genitalia) or 'gender blenders' (who exhibit a mix of characteristics attributed to either gender role).[43] 'Even transgendered individuals who decide not to have surgery, and who may blend genders comfortably, such as some of the female-to-males interviewed by Jason Cromwell, will usually say that they are men or women, not something in between, and not something different from both men and women.'[44]

Lang asserts that there are other cultures which not only recognize more than two genders, but also institutionalize gender variance, citing the Chukchi of Siberia who recognize as many as seven gender categories apart from men and women. And many, if not most of the North American Indian cultures traditionally recognize three or four genders including woman-man and man-woman.[45] Among the Northeastern tribes of the Plateau region of California, women-men perform 'women's' tasks such as cultivating corn, collecting firewood, spinning and weaving blankets and domestic work including raising children within the extended family. Lang notes that these women-men are also said to 'act like women' or 'behave like members of the opposite sex . . . adopting manners, gestures, and ways of moving or sitting exhibited by the women of their culture, but not by the men . . . (and) they will talk in a voice that is closer to a woman's than to a man's'.[46]

This phenomenon of the adoption of behavioural characteristics associated with the opposite gender is also evident amongst Albania's 'sworn virgins'. Another similarity between the two is that in many North American tribes, it is the family who decide to raise a boy as a girl. As in Albania, a 'culturally defined separate gender for females adopting men's work, garb and manners . . . still exists'[47] amongst certain North American tribes. The comparison ends, however, concerning sexual practise. Native American 'men-women' would usually have relationships or marriages with men although some are said to have remained single (others married women).[48]

There is however, some indication that 'sworn virgins' are not in every case treated absolutely on an equal footing with the men in their society. For example, Stana's request for a hunting licence and membership in the local shooting club was turned down even though she was an excellent marksman. Grémaux cites an anecdote in which Stana takes a turn in the local tournament and after watching the men repeatedly miss, 'much to the dishonour of the competitors, Stana's first shot hit the mark.'[49] There is a double standard here: if there is dishonour associated with a socially accepted 'male' beating an actual male at a male sport this would imply that there is in fact some hierarchical value system being imposed in which men still occupy a slightly higher position than 'sworn virgins', giving further evidence for these men-women as occupying an undefined middle ground, a third gender. However, one must be aware of cultural biases which could influence the choice of the word 'dishonour', which may have belonged to the author rather than the villagers.

Grémaux cites one more case where a 'sworn virgin' was not given completely equal status with a man: that of Tonë, a Catholic, buried in male dress, but refused the ritual lamentation by males normal among their tribe of origin (the Kelmënd), by the local Grudë tribe amongst whom Tonë and her brother had lived most of their lives.[50]

'In most Native cultures, the role involved crossdressing and taking on the vocational activities usually done by men, most notably hunting.'[51] Lang reiterates this, pointing out that in the instances where parents chose to bring up their daughters as boys, this usually occurred in regions where subsistence largely relied on hunting, a man's domain with the sexually gendered division of labour. If no boys were born into a family, or if all boys in a family had died, there was a need to socialize a girl to be a boy or man within the family.

Figure 32. Hajdar heads a family of seven in a neatly kept 2-room apartment inside a crumbling tenement block. Nick Cornish: Bajram Curri, 1995

All this evidence points towards gender as a culturally constructed concept. In societies that recognize more than two genders, 'the adoption of manners and work activities of the other sex cannot properly be termed a "gender reversal" – which implies exchanging one gender for the other within a two-gender system. Moreover, in many cases individuals grow up as members of a gender that is neither "man" nor "woman" from a very early age, which means that they never really "shift" from one gender to another.' Furthermore, a relationship between two members of the same sex but *not* considered of the same gender can therefore not be considered a homosexual relationship. 'The concept of transsexualism, which has developed in a culture that only recognizes the values of two genders and two sexes, is not applicable.'[52]

Notes

1. Connell, R.W. (1996), Masculinities, Cambridge, UK: Polity Press, p. 71.
2. Paglia, C. (1991), *Sexual Personae, Art and Decadence from Nefretiti to Emily Dickinson*, New York: Vintage, p. 201; quoted in Feldman, L.C. (1998), 'Engendered Heritage: Shakespeare's Illyria Travested,' *Croatian Journal of ethnology and Folklore Research*, vol. 35, no. 1, p. 223.

3. Wheelwright, J. (1990), *Amazons and Military Maids: Women who Dressed as Men in Pursuit of Life Liberty and Happiness*, London, Pandora, p. 8.

4. Wheelwright (1990), *Amazons and Military Maids*, p. 8.

5. The company was established in 1914 and now owns theatres in Tokyo and Takurazuka. It consists of five troupes.

6. Rogers, P. (1982), 'The Breeches Part', in Boucé, P.-G. (ed.) *Sexuality in Eighteenth-Century Britain*, Manchester: Manchester University Press, p. 249, quoted in Wheelwright, *Amazons and Military Maids*, quoted by Wilson, J.H.

7. Wheelwright (1990), *Amazons and Military Maids*, p. 9.

8. Wheelwright (1990), *Amazons and Military Maids*, p.11.

9. Wheelwright (1990), *Amazons and Military Maids*, p. 19.

10. Devor, H. (1997), *FTM: Female-to-Male Transsexuals in Society*, Bloomington; Indianapolis: Indiana University Press, p. 29.

11. Wheelwright, J. (1991), 'Captain Flora Sandes: A Case Study in the Social Construction of Gender in a Serbian Context', Chapter six in Allcock, J.B. and Young, A. (eds) (1991), *Black Lambs and Grey Falcons: Women Travellers in the Balkans*, Bradford: Bradford University Press; Republication (forthcoming 2000), Oxford; New York: Berghahn, pp. 82–9.

12. See for example: Wheelwright (1990), *Amazons and Military Maids*, p. 61.

13. Wheelwright (1990), *Amazons and Military Maids*, pp. 101, 145, 149.

14. They have sometimes been described as the Albanian 'Robin Hood and Maid Marion'.

15. Backer, B. (1979), *Behind the Stone Walls: Changing Household Organization among the Albanians of Kosovo*, Oslo: PRIO-publications S-8/79, p. 311.

16. Devor (1997), *FTM*, p. 35.

17. Williams, Walter, L. (1992), *The Spirit and the Flesh: Sexual Diversity in American Indian Culture*, Boston: Beacon Press.

18. Jacobs, S-E. and Thomas, W. (Nov. 1994), 'Native American Two-Spirits', *Anthropology Newsletter*, p. 7.

19. Phillimore, P. (1991), 'Unmarried Women of the Dhaula Dhar: Celibacy and Social Control in Northwest India', *Journal of Anthropological Research*, vol. 47, pp. 33–50.

20. Phillimore, P. (Forthcoming) 'Being a *Sadhin*: Celibate Lives and Anomalous Identities in North-West India', Chapter 6 in Sobo, E. and Bell, S., Madison, Wisconsin: University of Wisconsin Press.

21. Phillimore (forthcoming), 'Being a *Sadhin*', p. 6.

22. Haworth, B. (May 1993), 'Samoa: Where Men Think they are Women', *Marie-Claire*, p. 50

23. Haworth (May 1993), 'Samoa', p. 50.

24. Haworth (May 1993), 'Samoa', p. 50.

25. Haworth (May 1993), 'Samoa', p. 52.

26. Haworth (May 1993), 'Samoa', p. 52.

27. Haworth (May 1993), 'Samoa', p. 52.

28. Personal discussion, May 1999.

29. Wood, J.C. (1999 forthcoming), *When Men Become Women: Parallel Dimensions of Space and Gender among Gabra Camel Herders of East Africa*, Madison, Wisconsin: University of Wisconsin Press, p. 1.

30. Wood (1998), 'When Men Become Women', p. 1.

31. Wood (1998), 'When Men Become Women', p. 10.

32. Wood (1998), 'When Men Become Women', p. 12.

33. Wood (1998), 'When Men Become Women', p. 13.

34. Wood (1998), 'When Men Become women', p. 2.

35. Dickeman, M. (1998), 'The Balkan Sworn Virgin' in B. Zimmerman (ed.), *The Encyclopedia of Lesbianism*, forthcoming.

36. Wood (1998), 'When Men Become Women', p. 2.

37. Garber, M. (1992), *Vested Interests: Cross-Dressing and Cultural Anxiety*, New York; London: Routledge, p. 14.

38. Wood (1998), 'When Men Become Women', p. 27.

39. Wood (1998), 'When Men Become Women', p. 27.

40. Wood (1998), 'When Men Become Women', p. 28.

41. Bolin, A. (1996), 'Traversing Gender: Cultural Context and Gender Practices' in Ramet, S.P. (ed.), *Gender Reversals and Gender Cultures: Anthropological and Historical Perspectives*, London; New York: Routledge, p. 25.

42. Bolin (1996), 'Transversing Gender', p. 26.

43. Lang, S. (1996), 'There is More than Just Women and Men: Gender Variance in North American Indian Cultures', in Ramet, S.P. (ed.), *Gender Reversals and Gender Cultures*, pp. 185–7.

44. Lang (1996), 'There is More than Just Women and Men', p. 186.

45. Lang (1996), 'There is More than Just Women and Men', p. 106.

46. Lang (1996), 'There is More than Just Women and Men', p. 189.

47. Lang (1996), 'There is More than Just Women and Men', p. 191.

48. Lang (1996), 'There is More than Just Women and Men', p. 192.

49. Grémaux, R. (1994), 'Woman Becomes Man in the Balkans', in Herdt, G. (ed.), *Third Sex, Third Gender: Beyond Sexual Dimorphism and History*, New York: Zone Books, p. 261.

50. Grémaux, R. (1989), 'Mannish Women of the Balkan Mountains', in Bremmer, J. (ed.) *From Sappho to de Sade: Moments in the History of Sexuality*, London: Routledge, pp. 152–3.

51. Devor (1997), *FTM*, p. 27.

52. Lang (1996), 'There is More than Just Women and Men', p. 193.

8

The Changing World: The Challenge Ahead

'The vital factor in assessing transformation within the village community is the way local individuals assess changes that have taken place within their lifetimes . . . we can gain some insight into the meaning of change by looking at the differing ways in which discrete historical patterns of experience are evaluated.'

J.M. Halpern, *The Changing Village Community*[1]

Outside Perspectives and Influences

As Joel Halpern suggests above, in addition to the extensive social changes following the fall of Communism in Albania, further influences which are rapidly effecting change throughout Albania are brought through education, and employment abroad. The return of Albanians to native areas from working abroad, either on short visits or more permanently, is already having a great impact. With foreign media to back up their portrayal of modernity, such returnees question traditional mores. However, there have been fewer leaving northern Albania for these purposes, than from Kosov@ or other parts of Albania.

It continues to be true that more men than women pursue higher education, taking them outside their areas and even abroad, and from there they tend to move into jobs away from their native homes. However, those who return bring fashions which, either temporarily or permanently, affect the local populations, and are often considered to be superior. Fashion (even if only seen on television) will also have its impact on the population, especially the young people, in all spheres of life: not only will there be an increased demand for material goods, but attitudes to domestic behaviour and the emphasis on the family, will also be questioned.

Based purely on subjective observation, I would estimate that approximately one hundred 'sworn virgins' are now living, primarily in northern Albania. Some may go unnoticed, dressed as men; even those who know them may not be aware of their actual sex.[2] I have not yet met any child who is being brought up to be one of the next generation's 'sworn virgins'. The youngest was twenty-two when I first met her, living in a small town with her family. She seemed quite disoriented by the ambiguity of her role; she did not appear confident and assertive and was not very forthcoming in her discussion about her role, even though she agreed to talk to me about it. On meeting her a year later I found she had fully accepted her role (see Medi, pp. 85–87).

A 'sworn virgin' who has given a vow of celibacy is under extreme pressure and scrutiny to conform, consistent with the traditional laws of the *Kanun*. Whitaker writes of the northern Albanians that they: 'seem to be highly restrained in the overt expression of sexual emotion . . . indeed chastity provides one of the key concepts in the chain of rights which made up the ideal of family honor, on which the bloodfeud rested'.[3] Grémaux comments that, 'In transvestite Balkan virgins we see this inherent ambiguity and ambivalence substantially reduced by their classification as "social men", as well as by prescriptions and restrictions concerning their sexual behavior.'[4]

Clarification has already been made (in Chapter 4) that the 'sworn virgin' phenomenon, purely an exchange of gender role to fulfill a need within society, should not be confused with homosexuality. Albanian law on homosexuality has never referred to women: lesbianism is still barely discussed or properly understood even in Albania's capital. At present there lack role models for lesbians (supporting the argument of many Albanians that lesbians do not exist in their society).[5] On pursuing the topic amongst the inhabitants of northern Albania I was met with quizzical incomprehension and a reminder that the laws of the *Kanun* are strictly monitored. Any such feelings amongst the 'sworn virgins', though never discussed, could simply remain latent, if indeed the notion occurs at all to those who have chosen a life of strict celibacy. As Dickemann confirms, 'sworn virgins' are not treated as some intermediate third sex or gender, but rather that they are 'socially men'.[6] Moreover, as mentioned in Chapter 7 proscribing the 'sworn virgins' to a 'third gender', calling them transsexuals, transgendered or even cross-dressers are all concepts to which many Albanians, not least the 'virgins' themselves would certainly not subscribe.

Kosov@

Backer mentions that in Kosov@ it is acceptable for schoolgirls to claim that they 'want to be boys' and that 'by doing that and by announcing it publicly, i.e. to class-mates, they manage to exempt themselves from the common value judgements on female behaviour' and are easily accepted in this way by their class-mates. Backer understands this status to have 'something in common with the old "sworn virgin" institution – a transgression from one behavioural pattern to another in order to obtain rights belonging to the opposite sex. There is no suspicion of any "sexual deviance" thrown upon these females, as everybody seems to recognize the phenomenon as a purely social choice between different life styles.'[7]

While men left Kosov@ as migrant workers, although they continued to maintain strong links with their families, women were already forced to take on more of a leadership role: this was only seen as temporary. However, this change of gender roles amongst Kosovar Albanian families will affect family structure far more following their rapid uprooting and the killing of so many of their men in the late 1990s. Inevitably, traditional ways of life for those who return will be influenced by the conditions of their return. For those who remain in the many countries to which they have fled there will be other pressures. Many more women will now certainly have to take family decisions, but in their new environments this is unlikely to force them into the role of 'sworn virgins'.

One of the cases in Kosov@ (Raba, pp. 82–83) has been discussed and others have been referred to. The film *Virdžina* (see pp. 58 and 62) although ostensibly featuring a family living in Montenegro in the nineteenth century was inspired by the life of a 'sworn virgin' born in south-west Kosov@ in 1944. Shortly after the film was made, the prototype for Stefan received publicity, and radio and television interviews revealed that she had indeed been brought up as a boy, had done military service and served as a male on the local council. Although by the end of the film it is made clear that Stefan will not waver from the allocated male role, in reality she met a man (at council meetings) with whom she fell in love and married. One of their daughters has been a spokesperson for the family.

The break-up of Yugoslavia and the developing (anti-Albanian) nationalism encouraged by the Serb leader, Slobodan Milosević, exacerbated discrimination against Albanians in Kosov@ which grew into persecution. This resulted in some seeking a livelihood in the less oppressive environment of Albania. By 1998, the influx of thousands of refugees escaping from the war spreading in Kosov@ imposed a sudden, drastic change to a region already forced to live at little above subsistence level.

Noel Malcolm notes that Kosov@ 'is one of the cultural crossing-places of Europe . . . it became the geographical heart of an important medieval kingdom; it was one of the most characteristic parts of the Ottoman Empire in Europe; it was the area in which the modern Albanian national movement was born, and had its greatest successes and failures'.[8]

Northern Albania, with its historical and geographical affiliation with Kosov@ was most affected by the long-predicted eruption of systematic and continuous violence bringing a sudden influx of hundreds of thousands of homeless people. Inevitably this had a negative effect on development in Albania, although it once again brought humanitarian aid, and some reparation of the infrastructure in the areas in which refugees are most densely located. The refugees themselves were surprised to find the extent of poverty of the people living in the mountains of northern Albania. Despite living so close geographically to their neighbours over the border, communication was closed for half a century.

The terrible plight of Kosovar Albanian civilians resulted from the orders of Milosević, ostensibly under the guise of defeating the *Ushtria Çlirimtare ë Kosovës* (KLA, Kosova Liberation Army).[9] Albania, the poorest country in Europe, was the only one to positively welcome hundreds of thousands of Kosovar Albanians (by June 1999, more than one to every nine Albanian inhabitants). The strength of customary law and the strong traditions of the honour of hospitality ensured many refugees food and shelter in Albanian homes.

The massive and sudden arrival of so many people in chronic need has impacted strongly on the very fabric of Albanian society. Since most of the refugees are women and children, the need for men and household heads has been greatly increased. The influx of Kosovar Albanian families, so many of whose men have been detained or killed, combine to provide a context which Dickemann describes as 'one of the strongest motive forces in creating an institutionalized female-to-male role and making possible consensus among lineage members for each individual transformation'.[10] A possible outcome of the tragedy could be for some women to assume the role of 'sworn virgin' in order to compensate for the loss of male lives.

What will Become of the 'Sworn Virgins'?

There have been strong influences from outside the area both visually (through television) and physically, with the arrival of many foreigners including aid workers and religious groups. It seems likely that these will work to break down any social customs which do not fit in with such intrusions. The changes brought about by education may be tempered by the difficulties of serving an increased population, but more by lack of funding needed to provide new schools and equipment and for the re-writing of history. Education will certainly hasten the end of a custom whose redress for the servile position of women is to force them into celibacy. In Albania an additional factor which is likely to erode the determination of 'sworn virgins' to keep their vow is the increasingly wide desire to emigrate. When this eventually affects them, they may find that they can no longer retain their male status abroad but are forced by their exposure to Western culture to make compromises in order to adjust to their new surroundings.

As the two major reasons for women to become men – arranged marriages and male inheritance – are abandoned, so also the need for 'sworn virgins' will disappear. To counteract this possible trend, the re-emergence and upsurge of bloodfeuds in northern Albania, since the fall of Communism in 1991, could again place the same pressures on this society.

Members of the Women's Movement in Albania have discussed the situation of 'sworn virgins,' but consider them of little relevance to the Movement, since their unstated position actually reinforces the patriarchal system with which the Women's Movement is so much in contention. The 'sworn virgins' themselves neither know about, nor show much interest in the Women's Movement. It seems unlikely that the traditional values of 'sworn virgins' will accommodate to the very recently formed women's groups. Despite the rise of the Women's Movement in the last decade (see Appendix 3), in rural areas of northern Albania discussion of even birth control is still taboo. According to Djana Djaloshi there is still considerable support amongst women themselves to maintain *Kanun* law.[11] Modern Albanian governments have avoided recognition of the existence of traditions, including the laws of the *Kanun*. After 1967, and especially after the 'cultural revolution' of 1974, many antiquated customs were declared non-existent. Hence there were no official records sought or kept of women living as men.

With the erosion of the closely knit extended family structure, there will inevitably follow a greater demand for women's rights to be observed. Their rights to leave home, to get an education and to pursue careers from which they will probably not return to traditional family life, will in turn force further change in family relationships. Furthermore, it is likely that those who in the past might have turned to the tradition of becoming a 'sworn virgin', in the future will assert their rights in other ways.

This book leaves many questions unanswered, and intentionally so. Other than the brief statements in the different versions of the *Kanun*, those taking on the role of 'sworn virgins' have no firm guidelines. This traditional role will necessarily be forced to adapt to a changing world.

Notes

1. Halpern, J.M. (1967), *The Changing Village Community*, Englewood Cliffs, N.J.: Prentice-Hall, Inc., pp. 15–16.

2. There have been several tales of the discovery of the true sex only after the individual's death. An example is given by Grémaux quoting a 25-year-old: '"It was only after his death that I realized that Uncle Tonë had in fact been a woman"'; Grémaux, R. (1989), 'Mannish Women of the Balkan Mountains' in Bremmer, J. (ed.), *From Sappho to de Sade: Moments in the History of Sexuality*, London: Routledge, p. 151.

3. Whitaker, I. (1989), 'Familial Roles in the Extended Patrilineal Kingroup in Northern Albania', in Peristany, J.G. (ed.), *Mediterranean Family Structures*, p. 199.

4. Grémaux, R. (1994), 'Woman Becomes Man in the Balkans', in Herdt, G. (ed.), *Third Sex, Third Gender: Beyond Sexual Dimorphism in Culture and History*, New York: Zone Books, p. 246.

5. That the same is true in Kosov@ was brought home to me through a document produced to assist social workers in Britain in their understanding of Kosovar refugee women: 'I asked about homosexuality and people did not feel that it existed': Refugees Action (26 May 1991), *Kosovan Refugee Reception Centres: A Practical Guide*, London: Refugee Council. Section 3.1.6.

6. Dickemann, M. (1997), 'The Balkan Sworn Virgin: a Cross-Gendered Female Role' in Murray, S.O. and Roscoe, W. (eds), *Islamic Homosexualities: Culture, History and Literature*, New York: New York University Press, p. 201.

7. Backer (1979), *Behind the Stone Walls: Changing Household Organization among the Albanians of Kosovo*, Oslo: PRIO-publications S-8/79, p. 311.

8. Malcolm, N. (1998), *Kosovo: a Short History*, London: Macmillan, pp. xxiv–v.

9. Kosov@ (as also Vojvodina with a substantial Hungarian minority population) was made an autonomous province of Yugoslavia under Tito in 1974 with almost all the same rights of the six republics within the Federation. However, Milosević worked to dismantle this autonomy from 1987, repressing the majority Albanian population with increasing violence so that it became clear to Kosovar Albanians that only through independence could they be freed from oppression. For a decade they sought change through methods of nonviolence, before the escalating violence by oppressors and oppressed of 1998–9 erupted.

The author witnessed something of this repression when visiting Djakovica in September 1990 on the day that Belgrade authorities implemented their earlier conceived plan to revoke Kosov@'s autonomy. She witnessed the violent imposition of force in the face of a completely nonviolent response, little knowing how long the people of Kosov@ were to maintain such stoic strength.

Although the Dayton Accords did not address Kosov@, the outside world gradually focused on this area in Yugoslavia which was under effective military occupation since 1989, and since March 1998 under extreme and brutal attack.

M. O'Conner reported early on in the conflict (29 Aug. 1998), in his article, 'Disinherited Albanians on the Run for their Lives' in the *New York Times*, concerning one of the thousands of families forced to flee their homes:

PORNOC, Yugoslavia: Until last week (Gzim) Shala was the proud head of his extended family, owner of a house, livestock and equipment earned in twenty years of farming. Now he is one of (the) . . . ethnic Albanians driven from their homes by a Serbian offensive aimed at wresting control over central and western Kosovo . . . Shala's family ran through Serbian artillery, walked over mountains for four days . . . The youngest of his clan of sixteen is one, the oldest seventy-seven.

10. Dickemann (nd), m.s: 'The Balkan Sworn Virgin: a Traditional European Trans-person', p. 22.

11. Djaloshi, D. (Nov.–Dec. 1998), 'Northern Women and the Position between *Kanun* and Law', *Newsletter of the Albanian Civil Society Foundation*, p. 4.

Appendix 1

The 'Kanun'

The *Kanun* has long attracted the interest of foreign travellers and historians and more recently that of anthropologists and lawyers as well.[1] Marjorie Senechal draws attention to the importance of this *Kanun*, claiming it to be 'one of the world's great documents . . . endlessly fascinating'. She comments that 'its influence on Albanian society can be – very loosely – compared to that of the Bible in Western culture, where the deeply religious, the casual believers, and agnostics and atheists alike use biblical metaphors and parables almost unconsciously'.[2]

The Balkans, and Albania in particular, have long had the reputation of being wild and lawless. The derivative verb 'to balkanize' has come to be used in a derogatory sense meaning to violently fragment, disrupt or disorganize. Maria Todorova explains 'Balkanization . . . not only had come to denote the parcelization of large and viable political units but also had become a synonym for a reversion to the tribal, the backward, the primitive, the barbarian'[3] and further, how the Balkans have come to be described as the "other" of Europe. Vesna Goldsworthy pinpoints the moment when this 'other' was created as being the time when the Islamic rulers of previous centuries (perceived as enslavers of the largely Christian Balkan nations) lost their domination.[4] This perception is fuelled particularly by writers of the nineteenth century, especially such well-known poets as Tennyson and Byron.[5] Isa Blumi states that ' . . . a Western media culture that has a global, nearly hegemonic scope, has codified long out-dated notions of Balkan identity to fit a particular market niche'.[6] During the Communist period, the term 'Balkans' was dropped.

Albania, particularly the northern part, is seen as the last stronghold of tribalism in Europe; behaviour in the area by definition has been labelled primitive and warlike. Edith Durham pointed out however, that this behaviour is not so far removed from our own:

It is the fashion among journalists and others to talk of the 'lawless Albanians'; but there is perhaps no other people in Europe so much under the tyranny of laws.

The unwritten law of blood is to the Albanian as is the Fury of Greek tragedy. It drives him inexorably to his doom. The curse of blood is upon him when he is born, and it sends him to an early grave. So much accustomed is he to the knowledge that he must shoot or be shot, that it affects his spirits no more than does the fact that 'man is mortal' spoil the dinner of a plump tradesman in West Europe.

The man whose honour has been soiled must cleanse it. Until he has done so he is degraded in the eyes of all – as outcast from his fellows, treated contemptuously at all gatherings. When finally folk pass him the glass of *rakia* behind their backs, he can show his face no more among them – and to clean his honour he kills.

And lest you that read this book should cry out at the 'customs of savages', I would remind you that we play the same game on a much larger scale and call it war. And neither is 'blood' or war sweepingly to be condemned.[7]

The various versions of the *Kanun* laws were each named after well-known personalities in different areas or the areas themselves. Amongst them are the *Kanun* of Çermenik, the *Kanun* of Papa Zhuli, the *Kanun* of Laberia and the *Kanun* of Skanderbeg.[8]

Lek Dukagjini, the best known, was a wealthy chieftain and contemporary of Skanderbeg; he visited the Pope in 1466. The association of the name Dukagjini with the best-known *Kanun*[9] laws apparently relates to the fact that the area of their adherence is the same as that in which the Dukagjini family were especially prominent: the isolated northern Albanian mountain area defined by several ranges, steeply rising outside the borders of Albania itself into both Montenegro and Kosov@ to the north and east, and more gently to the west and south, within Albania. These *Bjeshket e Namuna* (Accursed Mountains) and other parts of the Northern Albanian Alps, form exceptionally rugged terrain whose people the Ottoman Turks, even during their 450 years of occupation of the rest of Albania, were unable to subjugate.[10]

During Ottoman rule, teaching and writing in the Albanian language were strongly discouraged and frequently forbidden. However, the oral tradition in the form of the Laws of Lek Dukagjini from well before the fifteenth century, lived on. Such has been the strict enforcement of the *Kanun*, that many aspects of life have remained little changed since his time.

Leonard Fox explains that these traditional laws of northern Albania, although not codified until the nineteenth century by the Franciscan priest Shtjefën Gjeçov, were considerably influenced by Illyrian law and were retained throughout the times of Roman domination.[11] Gjeçov initiated the first written form of the *Kanun* in 1913 by instalments in an Albanian periodical *Hylli i Drites* (Star of Light). He was murdered in 1926 before completing this work. Political motives have been attributed to the murder, connecting it to his having published in the Albanian language.[12] Gjeçov's work was completed by monks who influenced its bias. It was first published in 1933. In 1941 an Italian version appeared and in 1989 a lavish dual language (Albanian-English) edition was published. In 1993 the Albanian paperback edition brought easy access of the *Kanun* to the Albanian public.[13] Despite the harshness of some of the written laws, parts of the *Kanun* are taken very seriously. Kadare in his novel *Broken April*, voices the opinion of many through his character, Bessian:

> ... the *Kanun* is not merely a constitution ... it is also a colossal myth that has taken on the form of a constitution. Universal riches compared to which the Code of Hammurabi and the other legal structures of those regions look like children's toys. ... That is why it is foolish to ask, like children, if it is good or bad. Like all great things, the *Kanun* is beyond good and evil.[14]

Margaret Hasluck lived for over twenty years in Albania prior to the Second World War.[15] She was called on to brief British SOE forces before they parachuted into Albania in the War. She researched the intricacies of the *Kanun* during the 1930s and noted:

> The self-government of the Albanian mountaineers went far towards being true democracy in the Anglo-American sense of that much-abused word. In its primitive way it was really government of the People, by the People, for the People ... the legal system worked well on the whole, was often speedier and always cheaper than any European counterpart, and left few crimes unsolved.[16]

After the Second World War, Communist laws and propaganda were fairly effective in convincing many people that the *Kanun* in northern Albania was no longer respected. However, with the collapse of Communism and ensuing lack of any effective policing and judicial system, the revival of *Kanun* laws soon became apparent in its early area of control (northern Albania).

There is currently considerable debate concerning the influence of the *Kanun* and how far it has been romanticized (especially by foreigners) and manipulated by those who use it to justify murder.[17]

Notes

1. To mention only a few: Durham, M.E. (1909, 1985, 1987), *High Albania*, London: Edward Arnold: Republished and edited by John Hodgson, London: Virago; Boston, Beacon Press; (1928) *Tribal Origins, Laws and Customs of the Balkans*, George Allen & Unwin Ltd.; Peinsipp, W. (1985), *Das Volk der Shkypetaren: Geschichte, Gesellschafts-und Verhaltensordnung. Ein Beitrag zur Rechtsarchäologie und zur soziologichen Anthropologie des Balkan*, (The People of Albania: History, Community an Social Structure. A Contribution to the Legal Archaeology and Social

Anthropology of the Balkans), Vienna; Cologne, Germany; Graz, Austria: Böhlau; Pettifer, J. (1998), *Blue Guide: Albania*, London: A.C. Black; New York: W.W. Norton; Senechal, M. (1997), *Long Life to Your Children! a Portrait of High Albania*, Amherst, Massachusetts: University of Massachusetts Press; Thomson, I. (21 June 1992), 'Flesh and Blood in Albania', *Observer Magazine*; E. del Re and F. Gustincich (1993), *Pane, sale ecuore: il Kanun di Lek Dukagjini tra le genti delle montagne albanesi* (Bread Salt and Heart: the *Kanun* of Lek Dukagjini among the People of the Albanian Mountains), Bari, Italy: Argo; von Šufflay (1924), *Städte und Burgen Albaniens hauptsächlich während des Mittelalters* (Cities and Castles of Albania Principally during the Middle Ages), Vienna: Hölder-Pichler-Tempsky; Valentini, G (1956), *Il diritto delle comunità nella tradizione giuridica albanese* (Common Law in the Albanian Juridical Tradition), Florence, Italy: Vallechi Editore; von Hahn, J.G. (1854), *Albanesische Studien* (Albanian Studies) vol. l, Jena, Germany: Imperial Court and State Printery; Yamamoto, K. (12–16 Sept. 1994), 'The Tribal Customary Code in High Albania: a Structural Analysis of the Ethics', conference paper delivered to the Second International Congress on Physiological Anthropology, Keil, Germany; A. Young and P. Jani (Winter 1996), 'Traditional Law, Honor and Gender in North Albania and the Necessity of Reconciliation Processes', *Human Peace: International Union of Anthropological and Ethnological Sciences Quarterly New Journal of the Commission on the Study of Peace*, vol. 11, no. 1.

2. Senechal (1997), *Long Life to Your Children!*, p. 35. See also Schwandner-Sievers, S. (1999) 'Humiliation and Reconciliation in Northern Albania', in Elwert, G., Feuchtwang, S. and Neubert, D. (eds), *Dynamics of Violence. Processes of Escalation and De-Escalation in Violent Group Conflicts*, Berlin: Dunker & Humblot, pp. 130–1.

3. Todorova, M. (1997), *Imagining the Balkans*, New York; Oxford: Oxford University Press, p. 3.

4. Goldsworthy, V. (1998), *Inventing Ruritania: the Imperialism of the Imagination*, New Haven; London: Yale University Press, p. 11.

5. See for example Byron's *Child Harold's Pilgrimage*, Canto the Second; Tennyson's sonnet 'Montenegro' and from a Francisco Balagtas, a Filipino poet, in 1861: 'Story of Florante and Laura in the Kingdom of Albania' quoted in Senechal, M. (June 1998), 'Albania', *Sociological Analysis*, vol. 1, no. 2, p. 198; see also de Windt, H. (1907), *Through Savage Europe: being the Narrative of a Journey Through the Balkan States and European Russia*, London: Fisher Unwin.

6. Blumi, I. (Fall 1998), 'The Commodification of Otherness and the Ethnic Unit in the Balkans: How to Think about Albanians', *East European Politics and Societies*, vol. 12, no. 3, p. 535.

7. Durham, (1909, 85, 87) quoted in Robinson, J. (1994), *Unsuitable for Ladies: an Anthology of Women Travellers*, Oxford; New York: Oxford University Press, pp. 104–5.

8. Zojzi, R. *Kanuni i Labërise* (The Code of Laberia), Tirana: Institute of Folk Culture Archives); Illia, I.F. (1993), *Kanuni i Skanderbegut* (The Code of Skanderbeg) Shkodër: Botim i Argjipeshkvisë së Shkodërs.

9. Contributions were made in a panel discussion at the University of London on 13 February 1999, by lawyers, anthropologists and political researchers, on the value of these laws today. The collected papers are to be published as Albanian Studies Occasional Papers, no. 1, by the School of Slavonic and East European Studies.

10. Tax collectors sent by the Ottoman rulers were rarely able to penetrate the deep valleys and treacherous mountainside tracks to find the remote dwellings of Albania's northern mountains.

11. Fox, L. (1989), 'Introduction', Gjeçov, S. *Kanuni i Lekë Dukagjinit* (The Code of Lek Dukagjini), New York: Gjonlekaj Publishing Co., pp. xvi–xix.

12. Fox, L. (1989), 'Introduction', p. xviii.

13. Gjeçov, S. (1993), *Kanuni i Lekë Dukagjinit*, (The Code of Lek Dukagjin), Tirana: Albniform.

14. Kadare, I. (1991), *Broken April*, London: Harvill, Harper Collins, p. 73.

15. See Clark, M. (forthcoming 2000), chapter on 'Margaret Masson Hasluck' in Allcock, J.B. and Young, A. (eds), *Black Lambs and Grey Falcons: Women Travelling in the Balkans*, Oxford, New York: Berghahn.

16. Hasluck, M. (1954), *The Unwritten Law in Albania*, Cambridge: Cambridge University Press, pp. 11–12.

17. Several conferences have been devoted entirely to these matters. See for example papers (forthcoming) 'Albanian Studies Day "Custom and Law in a Time of Transition"' 13 February 1999, Albanian Studies, University of London.

Appendix 2

The Bloodfeud

Professor of Law, Ismet Elezi who has written extensively on the *Kanun*, lists many foreign writers who studied bloodfeuds in the century up to the Second World War.[1] The areas of Albania most affected by feuding are the northern mountainous areas where neither King Zog (in the 1920s–1930s) nor the Communists were able to eradicate the traditional method of revenge killing. Albanologist, Robert Elsie, comments that: 'at the beginning of the century (they) decimated the male population of entire regions of Northern Albania'.[2]

Whether the ritualized feuding which took place continuously in the north curbed population growth, or conversely whether population expansion caused continual pressure on the limited land and resources thus exacerbating feuds, is hard to tell. However, it is certain that the resulting violent loss of male lives at an early age contributed to the dearth of household heads.

The *Kanun* clarifies the manner and rights of retaliatory killing, in *gjakmarrje* (bloodfeud), in order to restore honour to the offended. As we saw in Chapter 3, the male household head (who may be a 'sworn virgin') takes responsibility for all decisions concerning its members. Thus he is also responsible for the family's decisions where honour demands any action to be taken in case of a bloodfeud. Many of the *Kanun* laws relate to the righting of wrongs, or thefts, and even insults, in order for honour to be upheld. The ultimate cost may be a man's life.

However, exactly *whose* life may not necessarily be specified. Such is the communality of tribal life that if a family member has been killed, honour is restored by killing *any* male member of the offending family. The manner and place of such pre-meditated killing is highly specified. For example the man who is killed in feud must be lain on his back by his killer, with his gun beside his head. There is no question of hiding the act of killing, since the main purpose is the public retrieval of family honour.

The *besa* (mentioned in Chapter 3) is an essential concept in the bloodfeud process. Articles 854–873 of the *Kanun* on the *besa*, relate to the proper conduct of a murderer and his victim family towards one another. The killer should pay respect to the dead man by attending his funeral: during that time a short-term *besa* is enforced ensuring that he is exempt from immediate retaliation.

Avenging honour involves the parties in a very systematic procedure. Honour is thought to be of far greater importance than life itself. Avenging 'blood' is not considered to be murder and the pride of those involved prevents anyone from seeking state or police assistance, which in any case would not usually be forthcoming. It is only men and boys from approximately eight years of age (an age at which they are considered capable of handling a gun), who are subject to killing.

'Sworn virgins' would expect to take a man's role in bloodfeuds. Whitaker suggests that by her acceptance of a change in gender relationship to the act of killing, 'by swearing perpetual virginity, and by assuming man's clothing, she could be treated socially as a man, and kill and be killed'.[3] All the 'sworn virgins' I spoke with asserted adamantly that they would be prepared to use weapons if the need arose; most, if not all, had easy access to lethal weapons.

Women's lives do not feature in retribution and a woman's presence is an inhibition to the act of killing. Honour may require that a mother remind her son if he is owed 'blood', that he should prepare to kill. In this way women are supporters of feuding. Traditionally the bloodied shirt of the one who was last killed, was hung in his home, to keep alive the urgency of retaliation.[4]

No man should be killed in his own home or, if a guest, by his host. Rose Wilder Lane recounts how her Shala guide delighted in taking her through the area of his rival Shoshi tribe, revelling in the hospitality his enemies had to show him in the presence of a woman. Had he been travelling alone, they would have shot him.[5] The only shelter that a man in feud can take is in his home or in a *kulla*, literally 'a fortified tower'. The only kind of windows that these stone buildings have are *frengji* (slits to fire a rifle from). Once in feud, all the male members of a family are potential victims who need this fortified lookout protection.

Edith Durham describes the function and occupation of one which she visited: 'The communal family lives in a kula, a great stone tower two or three storeys high. It has no windows, only holes for rifles. It is often perched on a rock for better defence. The ground floor is a pitch-dark stable. The entrance to the dwelling is by a flight of stone steps to the first floor.' At the time that she was writing, conditions within such homes were often very unsanitary:

An awful stench grips your throat. In pitch darkness you climb a wooden ladder to the living room up under the stone roof on which the sun blazes, making it as hot as a furnace. Thirty or forty human beings of all ages and both sexes are here crowded together ... The house is often filthy beyond all words. Though the painted chests ranged round the walls may be full of fine embroidered clothes for

Figure 33. A *kulla*: a stone tower house used for defence and retreat, whose windows are only large enough to fire a rifle through. This is the traditional home of families in feud, whose male members may not leave for fear of being shot. Some men live for years confined in such exile, unable even to go outside to tend their crops and cattle. AY: outside Bajram Curri, 1995

festivals, and silvermounted, the people are clad in dirty rags on which the lice crawl calmly. The little children are often naked. The . . . planks of the floor . . . are caked with dirt and saliva. Two sheep or goats are tethered in a corner fetlock deep in dung . . . through the floor rises the hot reek of ammonia from the stables, and you are scarcely seated before a black cloud of buzzing flies settles on you.[6]

It is extremely dangerous for any male member of a family in blood to leave his home. He would certainly be found, and probably killed by a member of the feud family, in any town in Albania. He might not be safe in any village, no matter how remote – it would probably only be a matter of time until he might expect retaliation. This has even extended on some occasions to male family members who have become targets in foreign countries.[7] But it has not prevented a few potential victims, fearing danger of retaliation, from seeking asylum in other European countries, Canada and the United States.

The majority of Albania's (approximately 10 per cent) Catholic population live in and around Shkodër, a town with an equal Muslim population. It was always the aim of the Catholic Church to put an end to the ritualized killing in bloodfeuds. Although church leaders have not succeeded in this aim, they may have prevented the rate from escalating even higher.

Despite the Communist propaganda, that the laws of the *Kanun* were archaic and had been firmly replaced, Aleksander Dardeli comments that 'what had seemed to be a sweeping success of the communist machine (has) sunk many people into a primitive existence controlled by a medieval mindset'.[8] By prohibiting its laws, Hoxha asserted that they had been eradicated and killing eliminated. It may actually have been the confiscation of land and property which checked bloodfeud killings.

But the laws were not forgotten, they persisted orally, and are now once again openly implemented. As Albanians 'awoke from the slumber of communism', Dardeli declares 'bloodfeuds continue to drain entire regions of northern Albania of their vitality'. Since 1991, all kinds of disputes, mainly in connection with land ownership, but also in other cases where honour was challenged or a *besa* violated, have caused hundreds, possibly thousands of killings in northern Albania.

Unfortunately the romanticized notion and status given to bloodfeuds through media attention, strengthens the resolve of all those who become involved in them since they perceive that their honour must be avenged not only in their own eyes and those of their neighbours, but also in the eyes of the outside world. It might equally be expected that reconciliation could benefit from media attention. However, the process of reconciliation is such a slow and sensitive one that those who negotiate between feuding parties are very cautious about allowing the delicate transactions to be observed by any not directly involved in them, in order not to jeopardize the ultimate aim of achieving a *besa* between the parties.

The new government of 1992 issued decrees authorizing the privatization of land and stock. It was stated that land should be distributed according to where people were actually living and the number in their family, with no reference to previous owners (only in the towns was there to be any recognition of previous owners, and they were to be limited by area). However, little clarification accompanied the decrees, nor were officials delegated to assist communities in following any procedure. Inevitably chaos ensued which manifested itself differently in different areas depending on the type of land, its previous use, earlier ownership, size of communities, etc. In some places authority figures were recognized and were able to organize some kind of fair system of distribution. In most places people were fearful of not being allocated their fair share and took what they could take while it was still available (particulary stock – much of which was killed and sold). The urgency of land distribution accelerated as the season for planting drew near. Some just staked a claim by fencing in a piece of land, clearing it of stones and ploughing it. These acts often led to an increase in feuding,[9] a situation which, as Fischer points out, has typically been engendered by each change of regime.

The Republican Party of Albania led a campaign against the new laws for a couple of years when many people signed a petition concerning the matter, but nothing changed. The question of land distribution is yet to be fully resolved. It is the cause of the majority of feuds. Disputes arise if a family is living on land which had belonged to another family prior to the Communist takeover after the Second World War. Even if a house was built within the last fifty years, it may be standing on land which belonged to another family. In some cases access to property crosses another's land and full negotiations do not take place or do not lead to agreement. Furthermore the population almost trebled in those fifty years, so that even if it were possible to share the land out as before, there would still be less available per person. Likewise in the towns, ownership of houses, apartments and stores was disputed. Added to this confusion was the total breakdown of already antiquated factories, the poor distribution of meagre medical supplies and the vandalization of schools and all means of transport. It is remarkable, however, that there was so little mass violence at that time.

Some bloodfeuds which recommenced following the fall of Communism, resulted from 'blood' owed from fifty years earlier.[10] This was the situation for a woman I visited in 1995. Ana had been a widow for the past sixteen years. Her husband had killed a man before the Second World War; in 1992 word reached her that the family of the man killed was placing a threat on her son. She was not personally at risk. However, from that time Ana's son and his young family stayed at home; he was unable to go out to work, the rest of the family live in constant fear. Their only income is from Ana's weaving which neighbours help her to trade.

The breakdown of the social and economic system has also fuelled a new kind of bloodfeud. The traditional feud, *gjakmarrje*, was a slow moving one. The taking of one 'blood' for one 'blood' can take months, years or even generations to effect. The other more modern version, *hakmarrje* (revenge over an ordinary offence) can lead to the more serious *gjakmarrje*. The *hakmarrje* however, does not adhere to all the old rituals, but rather to spontaneous 'justifiable' anger fuelled by the hopeless situation that so many find themselves in with the soaring cost of living, and few prospects for employment. These killings, although claimed to be traditional bloodfeuds, do not heed the controls of the *Kanun*, but use its existence as justification. Such a case is described by Ian Thomson in 1992:

> Murat and his son Kemal had gone to salvage the remains of a cowshed in the middle of a dissolved co-operative. It had already been agreed by other families in the village which parts of the property they could take. But father and son were ambushed, shots fired into the air as a warning. 'On 15 August, when my uncle set out again with Kemal for the village, I begged him not to go,' Myftar adds wearily: 'I followed close behind with a gun because Murat wasn't even armed.' Another ambush, and this time Kemal and his father were killed. The great engine of vengeance, the old idea of purification by blood, had now lumbered into motion. And Eduard Balia, as the eldest of three remaining sons, is bound by the *Kanun* to defend his family's honour at whatever cost.[11]

The *hakmarrje* also does not afford the traditional protection to women and children which the *gjakmarrje* always did, rendering them immune to the violence directed towards their families.

Although the traditional bloodfeud would not allow the shooting and killing of a criminal while a crime was being committed, with the recent social changes, the second form of less discriminating bloodfeud would certainly incorporate this as being a justified action. In either form of blood-feud (the traditional or modern), *all* male members of the extended family affected are considered equally valid as the next victim (traditionally it extended even to all male members of the *tribe*). State protection is totally lacking. First of all the central government does not wish to recognize the severity of the problem. Under Berisha's government, the opposition Party was blamed for exaggerating the problem in order to depose the government. The Socialist government, in power since 1997, has had to concert its efforts on the countrywide violence bequeathed by the earlier government as well as the major task of housing hundreds of thousands of refugees from Kosov@, further complicated by the actions of criminal gangs operating randomly all over the country.

When Berisha and his Democratic Party (voted in 1992) floundered and collapsed in 1997, it was found that many of its members were implicated in the fraud and smuggling. Many had become rich from the profits gained by illegally transporting oil through Albania. In the ensuing chaos, armouries were opened up and it was claimed that every man in Albania had obtained arms, a situation which inevitably exacerbated the violence of the increasing numbers of ongoing bloodfeuds.

There have been initiatives to resolve bloodfeuds as well as attempts to give people a new outlook, whereby honour need not necessarily demand killing, but might be attainable through negotiation, understanding and forgiveness. The National Mission for the Reconciliation of Bloodfeuds is a voluntary organization of elderly, experienced, revered men who work diligently to resolve feuds.[12] There have also been foreign initiatives attempting to support work with Albanians on mediation, with varying degrees of success.

Miranda Vickers reports that bloodfeuds were also still widely practised even under Yugoslav Communism amongst the Albanian population of Kosov@. However, contrary to the situation in Albania, Kosovar Albanians in the early 1990s, responding to increasingly oppressive Serbian rule, were much more ready to seek honourable ways to forgive one another and thus draw together in the face of the common oppressor. Vickers recounts an impressive attempt to break the cycle of feuds:

A concerted effort was made by enlightened students and Albanologists to stop the practice of blood vengence, which could be set off by such action as the killing of a sheepdog, an event which always started a feud. The process, which lasted a few months, resulted in reconciliation between some 2,000 families then involved in blood-feuds. About 20,000 men confined in their homes, since one feud invariably implicated all the adult males in a family, were consequently released.[13]

When reconciliation cannot be achieved directly between the two families, mediators are needed. The late well-known and charismatic folklorist, Anton Chetta[14] was active in mass reconciliations between Kosovar Albanians, ending the cycles of revenge. The gatherings were arranged in open spaces, including a football field, without public notice, but by word of mouth since this increased solidarity amongst Albanians and averted the risk of being discovered by the Serb authorities, which could invite further repression.[15]

The Bloodfeud in Literature and Film

Dritëro Agolli was one of Communist Albania's best-known writers. He headed the Albanian Union of Writers and Artists from 1973 until 1992. His writing conformed to the political requirements of the era, so that he could give the bloodfeud the appropriate connotations as an archaic tradition no longer practised. The hero of the novel, Mato Gruda is a peasant caught up in a feud at the time of the War of National Liberation. His conflicting loyalties form the basis of the story, and the conclusion is disappointingly predictable.

Ismail Kadare, now living in self-imposed exile in Paris, writes prolifically on matters pertaining to the history of his home country. His novels, usually set in Albania, can be read at several levels. His treatment of the *Kanun* in literature was unusual for the time when it was written. The evocative novel, *Broken April* (which was made into a film), is set in northern Albania in the early part of the twentieth century. A sophisticated literary-minded couple from Tirana spend their honeymoon in the wild vastnesses of the north, where their journey becomes intertwined with that of Gjorg, a young highlander caught up in the self-perpetuating mechanism of the bloodfeud.

By contrast Adem Demaçi's, politically controversial novel, *Gjarpit e Gjakut* (The Snakes of Blood)[16] which, at the time of writing, has not yet been translated into English, led Demaçi to endure years in jail. Miranda Vickers describes the novel as 'a powerful condemnation of the vendetta, the cruel social vice that haemorrhaged his own people'.[17] The novel became a popular and literary award-winning success, but also received government condemnation. This led Demaçi into opposition politics, resulting in twenty-eight years in Serbian prisons, earning him the title 'Kosova's Mandela'. Since his release in 1990, he has worked for the human rights of Kosovar Albanians and was awarded the Sakharov Prize for Freedom of Thought in 1991. He has become a strong political leader supporting some of the aims of the KLA, though not all their means.

Notes

1. Elezi, I. (1966), 'Sur la Vendetta en Albanie' (On the Bloodfeud in Albania), *Studia Albanica*, vol. 10, no. 1, p. 310. Elezi lists eight foreign Albaniologists who published work on bloodfeuds between 1899 and 1932.

2. Elsie, R. (1991), Review of Demaçi, A. (1990), *Gjarpijt e Gjakut* (The Snakes of Blood), Ljubljana, Yugoslavia: Lumi, *World Literature Today*, vol. 65, no. 1, p. 165.

3. Whitaker confirms this, using Ernesto Cozzi's work 'La Vendetta del sangue nelle montagne dell' Alta Albania' (The Bloodfeud in the Mountains of High Albania) *Anthropos*, no. 5, pp. 654–87, 1910: quoted in (1968), 'Tribal Structure and National Politics in Albania, 1910–1950' in Lewis, I.M. (ed.), *History and Social Anthropology*, London; New York: Tavistock Publications, p. 267.

4. See Kadare, I. (1991), *Broken April*, London: Harvill, Harper Collins, pp. 45–6. The Bankfield Museum in Halifax displays a piece of artwork interpreting

this custom, designed by Catherine Riley for the Museum's exhibition of the Edith Durham gallery.

5. Lane, R.W. (1922), *The Peaks of Shala: Being a Record of Certain Wanderings Among the Hill-Tribes of Albania*, London: Chapman & Dodd; New York: Harper & Bros., pp. 245–6.

6. Durham, M.E. (1910), 'High Albania and its Customs in 1908', *Journal of the Royal Anthropological Institute*, no. 40, pp. 462–3. I must comment that no matter how poor the homes I visited in Albania were, I was always struck by the remarkable cleanliness maintained inside, even under extraordinarily difficult conditions, both in the countryside and in the towns. Apartment blocks stand in grounds with no surrounding landscaping, often covered with litter and putrid heaps of garbage, yet hold within them homes maintained with care and pride.

7. Schwandner-Sievers, S. (1999), 'Humiliation and Reconciliation in Northern Albania: the Logics of Feuding in Symbolic and Diachronic Perspectives', in Elwert, G. Feuchtwang, S. and Neubert, D. (eds), *Dynamics of Violence: Processes of Escalation and De-escalation in Violent Group Conflicts*, Berlin: Dunker and Humblot, p. 135.

8. Dardeli, A. (4–6 Jan. 1997), 'Blood Feuds at the Turn of the Millennium: Time for a Farewell', *Illyria*, pp. 6–7.

9. A report by a Slovenian journalist, B. Jolis ('Honour Killing Makes a Comeback', published in the *Guardian* (14 Aug. 1996), translated from his article in *Delo*, indicates that as many as 50,000 people were involved and 5,000 killed by 1996.

10. For a more detailed discussion on these issues, see: de Waal, C. (1996), 'Decollectivisation and Total Scarcity in High Albania', in Abrahams, R. (ed.), *After Socialism: Land Reform and Social Change in Eastern Europe*, Providence, Rhode Island; Oxford: Berghahn Books, pp. 169–92.

11. Thomson, I. (21 June 1992), 'Flesh and Blood in Albania', *Observer Magazine*. See also Carver's description of the killing of a whole family of eight adults and twelve children in Bajram Curri in 1996: Carver, R. (1998), *The Accursed Mountains: Journeys in Albania*, London: John Murray, p. 252.

12. They are sometimes successful, but reconciliation is an extremely slow process and there are not sufficient workers, finances or resources to work on all the feuds currently in operation. The Mission members focus on feuds in which one party, usually the one who owes 'blood' has asked for mediation assistance. They are unable to provide protection: their members' only tools are words. The Mission's object is to mediate negotiation between the parties for an acceptable solution whereby neither side loses face. A further aim of the Mission is to change people's attitudes through education. Such also were the aims of the Peace Studies and Reconciliation Centre in Shkodër (founded in February 1995), whose members included several from the National Mission. The Centre had its office opposite the Rector's office at Shkodër University. Unfortunately with governmental changes in 1997, both the Rector and the Peace Studies Unit lost their positions.

13. Vickers, M. (1998), *Between Serb and Albanian*, London: Hurst & Co., p. 248.

14. For some details of his life, see obituary of Anton Chetta, by Prifti, N. (Spring 1996), 'A Great Mediator for Reconciliation: Anton Chetta 1920–1995), *Albanian Life*, Issue 59, pp. 41–2.

15. Discussion with Lala Meredith-Vula who was present at the largest of these gatherings in Verra të Llukës near Dečani, and helped direct the documentary film, *Forgiving the Blood*, shown on BBC TV, September 1992.

16. Demaçi (1958), *Gjarpijt e Gjakut* (The Snakes of Blood).

17. Vickers (1998), *Between Serb and Albanian*, p. 158.

Appendix 3

A Brief History of The Women's Movement in Albania

Women's needs in Albania are very different from those in, for example, the United States – they are different even from those in other former Communist bloc countries. Slavenka Drakulić, the well-known Croatian author has written extensively on this subject.[1] In the Albanian case, she blames television advertising for the destructive nature of Albania's revolution, and observes that the people 'are living in an illusion of a capitalist society, as they are living in an illusion of freedom or democracy'.[2]

Under Communism, women were theoretically equal to men. They were well-represented in government, though few at the highest levels. In certain spheres,[3] however, the Hoxha era did improve the lot of women: in education, in improved healthcare and the training of midwives. Whereas before it had been exceptional to give birth in the presence of a midwife, it now became more usual. The above factors combined to introduce a rapid increase in Albania's population. Hafizullah Emadi provides a glowing picture of the improved situation, commenting on the participation of women in government and other sectors of the economy.[4] Propaganda concerning the situation for women under Communism, however, did not give a true picture of their life at that time. Peter Prifti quotes Hoxha saying in 1967 that 'women are the most downtrodden, exploited and spurned human beings in all respects'.[5] In the same article, Prifti draws attention to the fact that in 1970 only two out of 119 government prizes for artists and writers went to women. Also, their 'equality' entitled them to work outside the home, but did little to change their role within the home.

The equality which Communism afforded women in fact meant that their workload doubled: as factory or manual workers during the day, and then having to take care of all the domestic work and childcare before and after their hours of official employment.[6] Furthermore, large families continued to be the norm during the Communist era, encouraged by Hoxha who wanted to increase Albania's workforce. Thus contraceptive devices and abortion were all illegal, bonuses being given to families for each newborn.[7] Since Communism fell, it has been a relief for some to have homemaking their only occupation. Forty per cent of all employes, but only 29 per cent of all managers, are women. Low female participation in public administration does not accurately reflect their level of education or skill, which is equal to or higher than that of their male counterparts.[8]

In the period 1960–90, the Union of Albanian Women had representatives in every community. Delina Fico, a leader in the Women's Movement labled this 'an explicit example of the governmentally organized non-governmental organizations (GONGO)'.[9] The only permitted organized women's groups were headed by Communist Party members or women of good political *biografi*,[10] thus preventing any trace of dissent from Party policy. The gender perspective was totally absent from public debate and it was very rare for women to discuss abuse or hardships, even if they had served time in political prisons or internment camps.

As Donert points out, 'the organisation of gender roles in Albania should not be seen as a barometer of its backwardness, but as a way of understanding how ideas about nation, history and tradition are constructed in Albanian culture'.[11] Priorities now for Albanian women lie in rights which women in the West assume as given. Many Albanians were reluctant to be identified with any group, so long had they been conditioned to view this as an illegal activity which could earn severe punishment. One of the first organized groups was the League of Ex-politically Persecuted Women, an important support group for women, some of whom had spent their whole lives in exile (in villages far removed from their own families) or in prison.

Albanian women are facing a wide range of problems exacerbated by the lack of long-term strategy and decision-making bodies for political, economic and social improvements. While laws are in the making, law-enforcement minimal and unemployment high, prostitution and trafficking of women are on the increase. There is very little provision for government support in cases of domestic violence, few women dare to report it, and on the rare occasions that cases are taken to court, they find negative responses – it is still men who are the judges. Abrahams comments, in his publication of 1996, that the Albanian government keeps no statistics on domestic abuse, nor is there any public campaign to raise awareness about the problem.[12] At that time also there were no battered women's shelters nor even any facilty for women to receive counselling. Since then there have been some initiatives in these areas. The problems may be partially offset by the respect that Albanian women have for one another in such a strictly patriarchal society. More recently protection from domestic violence is becoming an issue, but is not taken very seriously by Albanian men.[13]

Figure 34. Raba grinding coffee: only neighbours and family know her true identity.
Lala Meredith-Vula: Kosov@, 1995

Modern Albanian governments have avoided recognition of the existence
of traditions, including the laws of the *Kanun*. After 1967, and especially
after ther 'cultural revolution' of 1974, since many antiquated customs were
declared non-existent, there were no official records sought or kept of women
living as men. However, there was a rumour spread that in the area of Tropoje
in northern Albania, during the 1950s, several women took on the 'sworn

virgin' role as a form of protest against the Communist regime. Although this has not been substantiated, it is certainly true that this is the area in which I met the largest number, and visited a village which had been home to five within living memory. Likewise in the new 'democracy' after 1992, to accept that traditional laws still prevailed in any area would acknowledge a degree of weakness of state power and public security.[14]

Another matter of great concern is property rights. In this patriarchal society, especially in northern Abania where traditionally only men could inherit property, it has been more easily accepted that a woman should change gender than that a woman should inherit property in her own right. A few NGOs and associations concerned with gender issues have emerged, mainly in urban centres and organised by educated men and women.[15] Diana Çuli, a prominent writer and human rights activist, has had a major role in several new organizations: she is head of the Independent Forum for Albanian Women, founded in 1991, the year abortion was legalized. Amongst other groups formed in the early 1990s were the Interbalkanic Women's Association, the Albanian Nongovernmental Forum and the Albanian Helsinki Citizens' Assembly. The Democratic League of Albanian Women developed with the democratic movement, founded in 1991, estimated that it had 40,000 members all over the country, and branches in thirty-six towns. Its prime concern, representing the centre right political principles, is with decision-making in democratic reform in Albania in all aspects of political, economic and social life. This League, like the Forum of Republican Women and other party-affiliated women's groups, are concerned primarily with mobilizing women to vote for their party.

In 1995 the Women's Legal Group analyzed the draft labour law under review in parliament; many of their recommendations were adopted, thus providing the first legal women's rights. Fico considers that the World Conference on Women held in Beijing in 1995, attended by twelve Albanian women, was a turning point for their women's groups. By 1996, as many as fifty-five women's organizations were in existence. More recent issues are the harassment of women journalists, counselling on drugs and alcohol and provision of legal aid. Other groups serve as channels to distribute humanitarian aid. There is still a very great need for social and health services, especially for women.

Notes

1. See particularly her very amusing, but insightful collection of real life situations in: Drakulić, S. (1991), *Balkan Express*, London: Hutchinson.

2. Drakulić, S. (20 June 1994), 'Tirana Postcard: Bananas', *The New Republic*, pp. 16–19.

3. Instat (ca. 1998), *Femrat dhe Meshkujt në Shqipëri* (Women and Men in Albania), Tirana: Instituti i stotistikes, pp. 8–9.

4. Emadi, H. (March 1992), 'Development Strategies and Women in Albania', *East European Quarterly*, vol. 27, no. 1, pp. 79–96.

5. Prifti, P.R. (1975), 'The Albanian Women's Struggle for Emancipation', *South-eastern Europe*, vol. 2, part 2, p. 122.

6. Backer B. (1979), *Behind the Stone Walls: Changing Household Organization among the Albanians of Kosovo*, Oslo: PRIO-publication S-8/79, p. 314.

7. Post, S.E.P. (1998), *Women in Modern Albania*, Jefferson, North Carolina; London: McFarland, p. 133.

8. Instat (ca. 1998), *Femrat dhe Meshkujt në Shqipëri*, p. 8.

9. Fico, D. (April 1999), 'Women's Groups: the Albanian Case', *Journal of Communist and Transition Studies*, Special Issue: 'Engendering Change: Gender and Identity in Central and Eastern Europe', vol. 15, no. 1.

10. The *biografi* was the name given by the Communists to the political record kept on their citizens. Such record was affected not only by the actions of the individuals, but by those of their close family, and even by their extended and further removed ones. This form of control served to discourage attempted escape from the country (a treasonable offence). Many families were actually punished with imprisonment or internal exile (to a remote village far from their relatives) as a result of a family member leaving or attempting to leave the country. A good *biografi* reflected the praiseworthy actions of both the individual and those of relatives, in the service of the nation. A child with a good *biographi* was entitled to secondary and further education, leading to the possibility of more responsible and interesting jobs, possibly even with a choice of venue, whereas a bad *biografi* would bar all these possibilities for the holder.

11. Donert, C. (1999), *Trees of Blood and Trees of Milk: Customary Law and the Construction of Gender in Albania*, MA thesis, Albanian Studies, School for Slavonic and East European Studies, London University, p. 19.

12. Fred Abrahams interviewed Delina Fico of the women's group, Klub Reflexione, in Tirana. Abrahams, F. (1996), *Human Rights in Post-Communist Albania*, New York; London: Human Rights Watch, p. 131.

13. Several studies on the widespread practise of domestic violence have been carried out since 1992, for example see: Miria, S, Sala, V. and Fico, D. (1996), *Violence Against Women and the Psychosocial Taboos Favouring Violence*, Tirana: Women Association 'Refleksione'.

14. In the past there were cases where 'sworn virgins' were known to have registered officially in order to obtain their rights, for example Mikas was able to vote in parliamentary elections before the existence of female suffrage; see Grémaux, R. (1989), 'Mannish Women of the Balkan Mountains', in Bremmer, J. (ed.), *From Sappho to de Sade: Moments in the History of Sexuality*, New York; London: Routledge, p. 147. Selman Brahmin however (see p. 80) could see no advantage from governmental recognition; see Demick, B. (1 July 1996), 'In Albania, a Girl who Became a Man', *Philadelphia Inquirer*.

15. Donert (1999), *Trees of Blood and Trees of Milk*, p. 16.

Bibliography

Abrahams, F. (1996), *Human Rights in Post-Communist Albania*, New York; London: Human Rights Watch.

Agolli, D. (1983), *The Man with the Gun*, Tirana: 8 Nëntori. *The Albanians of Rrogam*, (July 1991), video made by Granada Television of England, series 'Disappearing World'.

Albanske Tradisjoner (Albanian Traditions) (1991), Exhibition catalogue from Oslo: Universitetets Etnografiske Museum, together with Oslo: Instituti i Kultures Popullore.

Allcock, J.B. and Young, A. (eds) (1991), *Black Lambs and Grey Falcons: Women Travellers in the Balkans*, Bradford: Bradford University Press. Republication (forthcoming 2000), Oxford, New York: Berghahn.

Amnesty International (1984), *Albania: Political Imprisonment and the law*.

Backer, B. (1979), *Behind the Stone Walls: Changing Household Organization among the Albanians of Kosovo*. Oslo: PRIO-publication S-8/79.

Bajraktarović, M. (1965–6), 'The Problem of *Tobelije*', *Glasnik Ethnografskog Museja*, Belgrade: Knjiga 28–29, pp. 273–86.

Barnes, R. and Eicher, J.B. (eds), (1992), *Dress and Gender: Making and Meaning*, Providence, Oxford: Berg.

Benzenberg, J. and Klosi, A. (1993), *Albanisches Uberleben* (Albanian Survival), Salzburg, Otto Muller Verlag.

Biber, M. (1980), 'Albania alone against the World', *National Geographic*, vol. 158, no. 4.

Birkett, D. (1989), *Spinsters Abroad: Victorian Lady Explorers*, Oxford: Basil Blackwell.

Bland, W. (1988), *Albania*, Santa Barbara; Oxford: ABC-CLIO Press.

Blumi, I. (Fall 1998), 'The Commodification of Otherness and the Ethnic Unit in the Balkans: How to Think about Albanians', *East European Politics and Society*, vol. 12, no. 3.

Boehm, C. (1984), *Blood Revenge: the Enactment and Management of Conflict in Montenegro and other Tribal Societies*, University Press of Kansas.

Bolin, A. (1996), 'Traversing Gender: Cultural Context and Gender Practices' in Ramet, S.P. (ed.), *Gender Reversals and Gender Cultures: Anthropological and Historical Perspectives*, London; New York: Routledge.

Bratanić, B. (1965), *Upitnica Etnološkog Atlasa* (Atlas of Ethnological Questions), Zagreb: Filozofski Fakultet u Zagrebu.

Bridge, A. (1945), *Singing Waters*, London: Chatto & Windus.

Bringa, T. (1995), *Being Muslim the Bosnian Way: Identity and Community in a Central Bosnian Village*, Princeton, New Jersey: Princeton University Press.

Buda, A. et al. (1989), *Kanuni i Lekë Dukagjinit: Mbledhur dhe Kodifikuar nga Shfjefen K. Gjeçovi*, Tirana: Academy of Sciences.

Buvinic M. and Youssef, N. (March 1978), *Women-headed Households: the Ignored Factor in Development Planning*, International Center for Research on Women. Report submitted to USAID/WID.

Campbell, J.K. (1964,74), *Honour Family and Patronage*, Oxford; New York: Oxford University Press.

Carver, R. (1998), *The Accursed Mountains: Journeys in Albania*, London: John Murray.

Clark, M. (forthcoming 2000), 'Margaret Masson Hasluck' in Allcock, J.B. and Young, A. (eds), *Black Lambs and Grey Falcons: Women Travelling in the Balkans*, Oxford; New York, Berghahn.

Coon, C. (1950), *The Mountain of Giants: a Racial and Cultural Study of the North Albanian Mountain Ghegs*, Cambridge, Massachusetts: Harvard University. Papers of the Peabody Museum, (1950), vol 23, no. 3.

Courtade, P. (1956), *Albania: Travel Notebook and Documentary*, London, Fore Publications Ltd.

Cozzi, E. (1912), 'La donna albanese' (The Albanian Woman), *Anthropos*, no. VII (Vienna), pp. 309–35.

—— (1910), 'La vendetta del sangue nelle montagne dell 'Alta Albania' (The Blood-feud in the Mountains of High Albania, *Anthropos*, no. 5, pp. 654–87.

Cusack, D. (1966), *Illyria Reborn*, London: Heinemann.

Del Re, E. and Franz G. (1993), *Pane, sale e cuore: il* Kanun *di Lek Dukagjini tra le genti delle montagne albanesi* (Bread, salt and heart: the *Kanun* of Lek Dukagjini among the People of the Albanian Mountains), Bari, Italy: Argo.

Demaçi, A. (1958), *Gjarpit e Gjakut* (The Snakes of Blood), Prishtina: Jeta e Re.

Denich, B.S. (1974), 'Sex and Power in the Balkans' in Rosaldo, M. Z. and Lamphere, L. (eds), *Woman, Culture and Society*, Stanford, California: Stanford University Press, pp. 243–62.

Dervishi, A. (1996), *Tales from the Wilderness: the Making of an Albanian Feminist Anthropologist*, MA thesis, University of Texas at Austin.

Devor, H. (1997), *FTM: Female-to-Male Transsexuals in Society*, Bloomington; Indianapolis: Indiana University Press.

de Waal, C. (1996), 'Decollectivisation and Total Scarcity in High Albania', in Abrahams, R. (ed.), *After Socialism: Land Reform and Social Change in Eastern Europe*, Providence, Rhode Island; Oxford: Berghahn Books, pp. 169–92.

de Windt, H. (1907), *Through Savage Europe: Being the Narrative of a Journey Through the Balkan States and European Russia*, London: Fisher Unwin.

Dickemann, M. (nd), 'The Balkan Sworn Virgin', MS.

—— (1997), 'The Balkan Sworn Virgin: a Cross-Gendered Female Role' in Murray, S.O. and Roscoe, W. (eds), *Islamic Homosexualities: Culture, History and Literature*, New York: New York University Press, pp. 197–203.

—— (1997), 'The Balkan Sworn Virgin: a Traditional European Transperson' in Bullough V. and B. and Elias, J., (eds) *Gender Blending*, Amherst, New York: Prometheus, pp. 248–55.

Djaloshi, D. (Nov.–Dec. 1998), 'Northern Women and the Position between *Kanun* and Law', *Albanian Civil Society Foundation Newsletter*, 17, p. 4.

Doder, D. (1992), 'Albania Opens the Door', *National Geographic*, vol. 182, no. 1.

Doja, A. (March 1998), 'Evolution et Folklorisation des Traditions Culturelles', *East European Quarterly*, vol. 32, no. 1. pp. 95–126.

Donert, C. (1999), *Trees of Blood and Trees of Milk: Customary Law and the Construction of Gender in Albania*, MA thesis, Albanian Studies, School for Slavonic and East European Studies, University of London.

Douglas, C.A. (March 1994), 'Albania: Feminism and Post-Communism', *Off Our Backs*.

Drakulić, S. (1991), *Balkan Express*, London: Hutchinson.

—— (20 June 1994) 'Tirana Postcard: Bananas', *The New Republic*, pp. 16–19.

Duka, V. (1995), 'Albania as Viewed by English Travellers of the Nineteenth Century', in Young, A. (ed.), *Albania and the Surrounding World: Papers from the British-Albanian Colloquium, South East European Studies Association held at Pembroke College, Cambridge, 29th–31st March, 1994*, Bradford: Research Unit in South East European Studies, University of Bradford.

Durham, M.E. (1909, 1985, 1987), *High Albania*, London: Edward Arnold. Republished and edited by John Hodgson, London: Virago; Boston, Beacon Press.

—— (1910), 'High Albania and its Customs in 1908', *Journal of the Royal Anthropological Institute of Great Britain and Ireland*, no. 40, pp. 453–70.

—— (1928), *Some Tribal Origins, Laws and Customs of the Balkans*, London: Allen & Unwin.

—— (1914), *The Struggle for Scutari*, London: Edward Arnold.

Edmonds, P. (1927), *To the Land of the Eagle*, London: Routledge.

Eicher, J. B. (ed.), (1955) *Dress and Ethnicity*, Oxford, Washington DC: Berg.

—— and Roach-Higgins, M.E. (1992), *Dress and Gender: Making and Meaning in Cultural Contexts*, New York; Oxford: St Martin's Press.

Elezi, I. (1966), 'Sur la Vendetta en Albanie' (On the Bloodfeud in Albania), *Studica Albanica*, vol. 10, no. 1, pp. 305–116.

Elsie, R. (1994), *Albanian Folktales and Legends*, Naim Frasheri, Tirana.

—— (1995), *History of Albanian Literature*, Boulder, Colorado: East European Monographs, no. 379.

Emadi, H. (March 1992), 'Development Strategies and Women in Albania', *East European Quarterly*, vol. 27, no. 1.

Erlich, V. (1966), *Family in Transition: a Study of 300 Yugoslav villages*, Princeton University Press, Princeton, NJ.

—— (1976), 'The Last Big Zadrugas: Albanian Extended Families in the Kosovo Region' in *Communal Families in the Balkans*, University of Notre Dame Press, Notre Dame; London.

Fico, D. (April 1999), 'Women's Groups: the Albanian Case', *Journal of Communist and Transition Studies*, Special Issue: 'Engendering Change: Gender and Identity in Central and Eastern Europe', vol. 15, no. 1.

Filipović, M. (1982) 'Women as Heads of Villages and Groups among the South Slavs and Certain Other Balkan Peoples' in Hammel, E.A. et al., (eds), *Among the People: Native Yugoslav Ethnography: Selected Writings of Milenko S. Filipović*, Ann Arbor, Michigan: Papers in Slavic Philology no. 3, Department of Slavic Languages and Literature, University of Michigan.

Fischer, B.J. (1999), *Albania at War, 1939–1945*, London: Hurst.

Fonseca, I. (1995), *Bury Me Standing*, New York: Alfred A. Knopf.

Forbes, R. (1944), *Gypsy in the Sun*, New York: E.P. Dutton & Co. inc.

Fox, L. (1989), 'Introduction', Gjeçov, S. *Kanuni i Lekë Dukagjinit* (The Code of Lek Dukagjini), New York: Gjonlekaj Publishing Co., pp. xvi–xix.

Garber, M. (1992) *Vested Interests: Cross-Dressing and Cultural Anxiety*, New York; London: Routledge.

Garnett, L.M.J. (1917), *Balkan Home-Life*, New York: Dodd-Mead.

Gilmore, D. (Dec. 1985), 'Introduction' Special Issue no. 3, Gilmore, D. and Gwynne, G. (eds), 'Southern Europe: Problems and Prospects,' *Anthropology*, vol. 9, nos. 1 & 2, pp. 1–9.

Girard, G. (July 1982), 'Notes on Early Photography in Albania', *History of Photography*, vol. 6, no. 3., pp. 241–56.

Gjeçov, S. (1993), *Kanuni i Lekë Dukagjinit* (The Code of Lek Dukagjini), Tirana: Albniform.

Gjeçov, S. (1989), *Kanuni i Lekë Dukagjinit* (The Code of Lek Dukagjini), New York: Gjonlekaj Publishing Co.

Gjergji, A. (1963), 'Gjurmë të Matriarkatit në disa Doke të Dikurshme të Jetës Familjare' (Traces of Matriarchy in some Former Customs of Family Life), *Buletini i Universitetit të Tiranës* (Shkencat Shoqërore), no. 2, pp. 284–92.

—— (1983) *Atlasi Etnografik Shqiptar (AESH): Përparjet në Veshjet Popullore Shqiptare (fundi i shek. XIX – mesei i shek. XX)* (Albanian Ethnographic Atlas (AESH): Aprons in Albanian Folk Costume (from the end of the nineteenth century to the middle of the twentieth century)), Tirana: Etnografia Shqiptare 13.

—— (1986) 'Aprons in Albanian Popular Costume', *Costume*, no. 20, pp. 44–62.

—— (1988), *Veshjet Shqiptare në Shekuj: Origjina Tipologjia Zhvillimi* (Albanian Dress Through the Centuries: Origin, Typology, Development), Tirana: Academy of Sciences.

—— (1994), 'Variations in Traditional Clothing According to its Function,' *Zeitschrift für Balkanologie*, vol. 30, no. 2, pp. 131–46.

Goffman, E. (1959), *The Presentation of Self in Everyday Life*, Garden City, New York: Doubleday Anchor Books.

Goldsworthy, V. (1998), *Inventing Ruritania: the Imperialism of the Imagination*, New Haven; London: Yale University Press.

Gordon, J. and C. (1927), *Two Vagabonds in Albania*, New York: Dodd Mead; London: John Lane, The Bodley Head.

Grémaux, R. (1989), 'Mannish Women of the Balkan Mountains' in Bremmer, J.

(ed.), *From Sappho to de Sade: Moments in the History of Sexuality*, London: Routledge, p. 143–172.

—— (1992), 'Franciscan Friars and the Sworn Virgins of the North Albanian Tribes', *Religion, State and Society*, vol. 20, nos. 3–4, pp. 361–74.

—— (1994), 'Woman Becomes Man in the Balkans' in Herdt, G. (ed.), *Third Sex, Third Gender: Beyond Sexual Dimorphism in Culture and History*, New York: Zone Books, pp. 241–81.

Grossmith, C.J. (1976), 'The Cultural Ecology of Albanian Extended Family Households in Yugoslav Macedonia, in Byrnes R.F. (ed.), *Communal Families in the Balkans: the Zadruga: Essays by Philip E. Mosely and Essays in his Honor*, Notre Dame, Indiana; London: University of Notre Dame Press.

Hall, D. (1994), *Albania and the Albanians*, London: Pinter.

Halliday, J. (ed.) (1990), *The Artful Albanian: Memoirs of Enver Hoxha*, London: Chatto & Windus.

Halpern, J.M. (1956), *A Serbian Village*, New York; Evanston; London: Harper Colophon, Harper & Row.

—— (1967), *The Changing Village Community*, Englewood Cliffs, N.J.: Prentice-Hall, Inc.

—— and Anderson, D. (1970), 'The *Zadruga*: a Century of Change', *Anthropologica*, vol. 12, no. 1, pp. 83–97.

Hammond, N.G.L. (1983), 'Travels in Epirus and South Albania Before World War II', *Ancient World*, vol. 8, pp. 13–46.

Hasluck, M. and Myres. J.L. (Dec. 1933), 'Bride Price in Albania: A Homeric Parallel', *Man*, vol. 3, pp. 191–5.

—— (1954), *The Unwritten Law in Albania*, Cambridge: Cambridge University Press.

Herbert, A. (nd), *Ben Kedim: a Record of Eastern Travel*, London: Hutchinson.

Herdt, G. (ed.) (1994), *Third Sex, Third Gender: Beyond Sexual Dimorphism in Culture and History*, New York: Zone Books.

Hibbert, R. (1991), *Albania's National Liberation Struggle: the Bitter Victory*, London: Pinter, New York: St. Martin's Press.

Hodgkinson, H. (1995), 'Edith Durham and the Formation of the Albanian State', in Young, A. (ed.), *Albania and the Surrounding World: Papers from the British-Albanian Colloquium, South East European Studies Association held at Pembroke College, Cambridge, 29th–31st March, 1994*, Bradford: Research Unit in South East European Studies, University of Bradford.

Hodgson, J. (Feb. 1998), 'Albania's Struggling Literary Scene', *Transitions*, vol. 5, no. 2, pp. 30–6.

Holtz, W.V. (1993), *A Ghost in the Little House*, Columbia, Missouri: University of Missouri Press.

Hudhri, F. (1990), *Albania and Abanians in World Art*, Athens: Christos Giovanis A.E.B.E.

Hutchings, R. (1996), *Historical Dictionary of Albania* (European Historical Dictionaries, no. 12), Lanham, Md.; London: The Scarecrow Press Inc.

Hyman, S. (1988), *Edward Lear in the Levant*, John Murray.

Illia, I.F. (1993), *Kanuni i Skanderbegut* (The Code of Skanderbeg), Shkodër: Botim i Argjipeshkvisë së Shkodërs

Index on Censorship (1994–8) issues concerning Albania.

Instat (ca. 1998), *Femrat dhe Meshkujt në Shqipëri* (Women and Men in Albania), Tirana: Instituti i Statistikes.

Isai, K. (ed.) (1990), *Brenga e Balkanit: dhe vepra te tjera per Shqiperine dhe Shqiptaret* (The Burden of the Balkans: and other works on Albania and Albanians), Tirana: Shtepia Botuese.

Jacobs, S-E. and Thomas, W. (Nov. 1994), 'Native American Two- Spirits', *Anthropology Newsletter*, p. 7.

Jacques, E.E. (1995), *The Albanians: an Ethnic History from Prehistoric Times to the Present*, Jefferson, North Carolina; London: McFarland & Company, Inc.

Jones, L. (1993), *Biografi: an Albanian Quest*, Andre Deutsch.

Kadare, I. (1991), *Broken April*, London: Harvill, Harper Collins.

—— (1995), *Albanie: Visage des Balkans. Ecrits de Lumière* (Albania: Face of the Balkans. Writing with Light), Photographs by Marubi, P., K. and G.; text translated from the Albanian by Vrioni, J. and Zbynovsky, E., Paris: Arthaud.

—— (1997), *The File on H*, translated by David Bellow from the French version of the Albanian by Jusuf Vrioni, London: The Harvill Press.

—— (1994), *The Concert*, translated from French by B. Bray, New York: William Morrow.

Karanović, S. (1991), (film) *Virdžina*.

Kaser, K. (1994), 'The Balkan Joint Family Household: Seeking its Origins', *Continuity and Change*, vol. 9, no. 1, pp. 45–68.

—— (1994), 'Die Mannfrau in den Patriarchalen Gesellschaften des Balkans und der Mythos vom Matriarchat' (Woman as Honorary Man in the Patriarchal Societies of the Balkans and the Myth of Matriarchy), *L'Homme Zeitschrift für Feministische Geschichtswissenschaft*, vol. 5, no. 1, pp. 59–77.

—— (1992), 'The Origins of Balkan Patriarchy', *Modern Greek Studies Yearbook*, vol. 8.

Kloep, M. and Nauni, A. (2–4 June 1994) 'Girls' Rebellion Against Patriarchal Society: Value Change in Albania', paper presented at the 4th Nordic Youth Research Symposium, Stockholm, Sweden.

Kusovac, Z. (Sept. 1998), 'Round Two: Serbian Security Forces: The Kosovo Liberation Army is Down but not Out', *Transitions*, vol. 5, no. 9, pp. 22–4.

Lane, R.W. (1922), *The Peaks of Shala: Being a Record of Certain Wanderings Among the Hill-Tribes of Albania*, London: Chapman & Dodd; New York: Harper & Bros. Translated into Albanian: Lein, R.U. (1997), *Majat e Shalës*, Prishtina Rilindja.

Lear, E. with introduction by Runciman, S. (1988), *Journals of a Landscape Painter in Greece and Albania*, Hutchinson.

Lévi-Strauss, C. (1978), *Structural Anthropology*, London: Penguin Books.

MacKenzie, G. and Irby, A. (1866), *Travels in the Slavonic Provinces of Turkey-in-Europe*, London: Alexander Straham.

Malcolm, N. (1998), *Kosovo: a Short History*, London: Macmillan.

Mayhew, A. (1881), 'In Albania with the Ghegs', *Scribner's Monthly*, vol. XXI.

Melman, B. (1992), *Women's Orients: English Women and the Middle East, 1718–1918*, Ann Arbor, Univ. of Michigan Press.

Miller, E.C. (1929), *Pran of Albania*, Garden City, New York: Doubleday, Doran & Co. Inc.

Miria, S., Sala, V. and Fico, D. (1996), *Violence Against Women and the Psychosocial Taboos Favouring Violence*, Tirana: Women Association 'Refleksione'.

Moore, H.L. (1994), *A Passion for Difference: Essays in anthropology and gender*, Indiana University Press, Bloomington and Indianapolis.

Munro, A. (27 June–4 July 1994), 'The Albanian Virgin', *New Yorker* pp. 118–38; also published (1994) *Open Secrets*, New York: Chatto, pp. 81–128.

Naval Intelligence Division (1945), *Geographical Handbook: Albania*.

Newman, B. (1936), *Albanian Backdoor*, London: Jenkins.

Oosthuizen, P. (1993), 'Private Feuds and Public Hangings: What Prospects for an Open Society in Albania?', *Albanian Life*, no. 1.

Ortner, S.B. (1981), *Sexual Meaning: the Cultural Construction of Gender and Sexuality*, Cambridge, Cambridge University Press.

Paglia, C. (1991), Sexual Personae, Art and Decadence from Nefretiti to Emily Dickinson, New York: Vintage, p. 201; quoted in Feldman, L.C. (1998), 'Engendered Heritage: Shakespeare's Illyria Travested,' Croatian Journal of ethnology and Folklore Research, vol. 35, no. 1, p. 223.

Peacock, W. (1914), *Albania: The Foundling State of Europe*, London: Chapman & Hall Ltd.

Peristiany, J.G. (ed.) (1965), *Honour and Shame: The Values of Mediterranean Society*, London: Wiedenfeld & Nicolson.

Pettifer, J. (1998), *Albania*, London: A.C. Black; New York: W.W. Norton.

Phillimore, P. (forthcoming 2000), 'Private Lives and Public Identities: an Example of Female Celibacy in Northwest India' in Sobo, E. and Bell, S. (eds), *Celibacy, Culture and Society: the Anthropology of Sexual Abstinence*, Madison, Wisconsin: University of Wisconsin Press.

—— (1991), 'Unmarried Women of the Dhaula Dhar: Celibacy and Social Control in Northwest India', *Journal of Anthropological Research*, vol. 47, pp. 33–50.

Pichler, R. (11 June 1999), 'History and Tradition: Producing Myths of the "Pure" National Character,' conference paper 'Myths in the Politics of Transition', Albanian Studies, University of London.

Post, S.E.P. (1998), *Women in Modern Albania*, Jefferson, North Carolina; London: McFarland.

Pouqueville, F.-C.-H.-L. (1826), *Travels in Epirus, Albania Macedonia and Thessaly*, London: Richard Phillips.

Prifti, P.R. (1975), 'The Albanian Women's Struggle for Emancipation', *Southeastern Europe*, vol. 2, no. 2, pp. 109–29.

Ramet, S.P. (ed.) (1996), *Gender Reversals and Gender Cultures: Anthropological and Historical Perspectives*, London; New York: Routledge.

Refugee Action (26 May 1999), *Kosovan Refugee Reception Centres: A Practical Guide*, London: Refugee Council.

Reineck, J. (1991), *The Past as Refuge: Gender, Migration and Ideology among the Kosova Albanians'*, Ph.D thesis, University of California at Berkeley.

Robinson, Vandeleur (1941), *Albania's Road to Freedom*, London: Allen & Unwin.

Rosenberg, T. (Winter 1994–95), 'Albania: The Habits of the Heart', *World Policy Journal*, vol. XI, no. 4.

Roux, M. (1992), *Les albanais en Yougoslavie: Minorité Nationale, Territoire et Developpement* (Albanians in Yugoslavia: National Minority, Territory and Development), Paris: Editions de la maison des Sciences de l'Homme.

Sandes, F. (1916), *An English Woman-Sergeant in the Serbian Army*, London, New York, Toronto: Hodder & Stoughton.

Sarner, H. (1997), *Rescue in Albania: One Hundred Percent of Jews in Albania Rescued from Holocaust*, Cathedral City, California: Brunswick Press; Boston, Massachusetts: The Frosina Foundation.

Schwandner, S. (1992), 'Albania', *Encyclopedia of World Cultures*, vol. 4. Bennet, L.A. (ed.), pp. 3–8. Boston: G.K. Hall & Co.

Schwandner-Sievers, S. (1999), 'Humiliation and Reconciliation in Northern Albania: the Logics of Feuding in Symbolic and Diachronic Perspectives,' in Elwert, G. Feuchtwang, S. and Neubert, D. (eds), *Dynamics of Violence: Processes of Escalation and De-escalation in Violent Group Conflicts*, Berlin: Dunker and Humblot, pp. 127–45.

Scriven, Brig. Gen. G.P. (Aug. 1918), 'Recent Observations in Albania'. *The National Geographic Magazine*.

Senechal, M. (1997), *Long Life to Your Children! a Portrait of High Albania*, Amherst, Massachussets: University of Massachussets Press.

Shryock, A.J. (Jan. 1988), 'Autonomy, Entanglement, and the Feud: Prestige Structures and Gender Values in Highland Albania', *Anthropological Quarterly*, vol 61, no. 1, pp. 113–18.

Sjöberg, Ó. (1991), *Rural Change and Development in Albania*, San Francisco; Oxford: Westview Press.

—— (1995), 'Macedonia's Mute Women in Waiting', *The Observer*.

Stahl, P.H. (1986), 'The Albanians' (ch. III) *Household, Village and Village Confederation in Southeastern Europe*, Boulder, Colorado: East European Monographs (no. 200), pp. 88–137.

—— (1991), 'Maison et groupe domestique étendu: exemples européens' (House and Extended Family: European Examples) in T. Timitkos (ed.) *Armos*, Thessalonika: Université Aristotèles, Ecole Polytechnique, p. 1,667–92.

Start, L.E. (1977), *The Durham Collection of Garments and Embroideries from Albania and Yugoslavia*, Halifax: Caulderdale Museums.

Swire, J. (1937), *King Zog's Albania*, London: Robert Hale.

Tarifa, F. (June 1998), 'East European Puzzles: Old and New', *Sociological Analysis*, vol. 1, no. 2, pp. 61–76.

—— (Sept. 1998), 'Making Sociological Sense of *Lamerica*', *Sociological Analysis*, vol. 1, no. 3, pp. 161–9.

Theroux, P. (1995), *The Pillars of Hercules: a Grand Tour of the Mediterranean*, London: Hamish Hamilton.

Thompson, E. (ed.) (1948), *The Railway: an Adventure in Construction*, London: The British-Yugoslav Association.

Todorova, M. (1997), *Imagining the Balkans*, New York; Oxford: Oxford University Press.

Vaka, D. (1917), *The Heart of the Balkans*, New York, Boston: Houghton Mifflin.

Valentini, G. (1943), 'La Familija nel Diritto Tradizionale albanese' (The family according to Traditional Albanian Law), *Annali Laternanensi*, vol. 9, pp. 9–219.

Van der Pol, H. (1992), *Estimation of the Level of Infant Mortality (preliminary analysis)*, Report prepared for the United Nations Fund for Population Activities, quoted in Senturia, K.D.W. (Oct. 1996), 'Maternal and Child Health in Albania', *Social Science and Medicine*, vol. 43, no. 7, pp. 1,097–107.

Van Hal, T. (1991), *Reizen en Schrijven: een Onderzoek naar het Werk van Mary Edith Durham* (Travel and Text: the Writings of Mary Edith Durham). MA thesis, University of Amsterdam, Netherlands.

Vickers, M. (1995), *The Albanians: a Modern History*, London, I.B.Tauris.

—— (1998), *Between Serb and Albanian: A History of Kosovo*, London: Hurst & Co.

Vince-Pallua, J. (1996), 'Introducing a Second Wife: a Matrimonial Lid in Cases of a Childless Marriage', *International Journal of Anthropology*, vol. 11, no. 1, pp. 35–40.

Vokopola, K. (1968), 'The Albanian Customary Law', *Quarterly Journal of the Library of Congress*, vol. 25, part 4, pp. 306–16.

Vukanović, T. (1961), 'Virdžine' (Virgins), *Glasnik Muzeja Kosova i Metohije*, VI, Prishtina, pp. 79–112.

West, R. (1982), *Black Lamb and Grey Falcon: a Journey Through Yugoslavia*, London: Macmillan. (First published in 1941).

Wheelwright, J. (1989), *Amazons and Military Maids: Women Who Dressed as Men in Pursuit of Life Liberty and Happiness*, London: Pandora.

—— (1991), 'Captain Flora Sandes: a Case Study in the Social Construction of Gender in a Serbian Context' in Allcock, J. and Young, A., *Black Lambs and Grey Falcons: Women Travellers in the Balkans*, Bradford: Bradford University Press. Republication (forthcoming 2000), Oxford; New York: Berghahn.

Whitaker, I. (1981), 'A Sack for Carrying Things: the Traditional Role of Women in Northern Albanian Society' in *Anthropological Quarterly*, vol. 54, no. 3, pp. 146–56.

—— (1989), 'Familial Roles in the Extended Patrilineal Kingroup in Northern Albania' in Peristiany, J.G. (ed.), *Mediterranean Family Structures*, Cambridge; London; New York; Melbourne: Cambridge University Press, pp. 195–203.

—— (1968), 'Tribal Structure and National Politics in Albania, 1910–1950', in Lewis, I.M., *History and Social Anthropology*, London; New York, Tavistock Publications, pp. 253–93.

White, L. and Dawson, A. and P. (1995), *Albania: a Guide and Illustrated Journal*,

Chalfont St Peter, Buckinghamshire, UK, Old Saybrook, Conn., Bradt Publications, Old Perquot Press Inc.

Wilkes, J. (1992), *The Illyrians*, Oxford; Cambridge, Massachusetts: Blackwell.

Williams, W.L. (1986), *The Spirit and the Flesh: Sexual Diversity in American Indian culture*, Boston: Beacon Press.

Winnifrith, T. (ed.) (1992), *Perspectives on Albania*, Hampshire and London: Macmillan.

Wood, J.C. (1999 forthcoming), *When Men Become Women: Parallel Dimensions of Space and Gender among the Gabra Camel Herders of East Africa*.

Yamamoto, K. (19–21 Jan. 1995), 'A Japanese View of "The Code"', *Illyria*, vol. 5, no. 365, p. 7.

—— (1999) 'The Origin of Ethics and Social Order in a Society Without State Power', Conference paper, Fourth International Congress on Physiological Anthropology, Zagreb, *Collegium Anthropologicum*, vol. 23, no. 1, pp. 221–29.

Young, A. (1998), *Albania*, World Bibliographical Series, Santa Barbara; Oxford: ABC-CLIO Press.

—— (1991), 'Rose Wilder Lane, 1886–1968', chapter nine in Allcock, J.B. and Young, A. (eds), *Black Lambs and Grey Falcons: Women Travellers in the Balkans*, Bradford: Bradford University Press. Republication (forthcoming 2000), Oxford; New York: Berghahn.

—— (Jan. 1999), 'Religion and Society in Present-Day Albania', *Journal of Contemporary Religion*, vol. 14, no. 1, pp. 5–16.

—— (Dec. 1995), 'Sworn Virgins of Albania', *Cosmopolitan*, pp. 44–8.

—— (Spring 1998), '"Sworn Virgins": Cases of Socially Accepted Gender Change', *The Anthropology of East Europe Review*, vol. 16, no. 1, pp. 41–49.

—— (1996), 'The Sworn Virgins of Albania', *Swiss Review of World Affairs*, Zurich: Neue Zürcher Zeitung, pp. 11–13.

Zaimi, N. (1937), *Daughter of the Eagle*, New York, Ives Washburn, inc.

Newspaper articles

Abrahams, F., (Fall 1994), 'Albanian Odyssey: Quest for the Albanian Virgin' *Slant*, New York: University of Columbia, pp. 14–16.

Baxhaku, F. (21 May 1996), '"Ja Përse Preferova të Jetoj si një Mashkull"' (Why I Prefer to Live as a Man), *Gazeta Shqiptare*, p. 7.

Benfield, C. (20 May 1995), 'Sworn Virgins in a Man's World', *Yorkshire Post*.

Binder, D. (11 Nov. 1994), 'A Code that Defines Albania has a Mixed Role in Shaping a Legal System for that Country', *New York Times*, B20.

Birkett, D. (5 Aug. 1999), 'Mutilation Won't Make a Man a Woman', *The Guardian*, G2, p. 5.

Dardeli, A. (4–6 Jan. 1997), 'Blood Feuds at the Turn of the Millennium: Time for a Farewell', *Illyria*, pp. 6–7.

Deligiannis, P.P. (16–18 Aug. 1997) 'A Day in the Life of an Albanian Woman', *Illyria*, p. 4.

Demick, B. (1 July 1996), 'In Albania, a Girl who Became a Man,' *Philadelphia Inquirer*.

Facchi, L. (20 Oct. 1998), 'Virgjëreshat e Shndërrura në Burra: Pashku, Lula dhe Xhema Tregojnë Historinë e Jetës së tyre' (Virgins Changed into Men: Pashke, Lule and Xhema Tell their Life Stories), *Shekulli*, p. 19.

Freedman, S. (17 Nov. 1996), 'En kvinnes liv som man' (The Life of a Woman as a Man), *Aftenposten*.

—— (3 Nov. 1996), 'Self Made Men', *Independent on Sunday*.

Haworth, B. (May 1993), 'Samoa: Where Men Think they are Women', *Marie-Claire*.

Jolis, B. (14 Aug. 1996), 'Honour Killing Makes a Comeback', *Guardian* translated from *Delo*, (a Slovenian weekly).

Narayan, N. (29 Aug. 1992), 'On Albanian Bloodfeuds', *Independent Magazine*.

O'Connor, M. (29 Aug. 1998), 'Disinherited Albanians on the Run for Their Lives', *New York Times*.

Pagani, S. (3–5 June 1996), '"Vowed Virgins" Keep Countryside Under Control', *Illyria*, p. 4.

—— (7 May 1996), 'Albania's "Avowed Virgins" Wear the Trousers', *Guardian*.

Parfitt, T. (1 June 1997), 'Land Beyond Time', *Spectrum*, p. 2.

Perlez, J. (15 April 1998), 'Blood Feuds Draining a Fierce Corner of Albania', *International Herald Tribune*.

Reineck, J. (17–19 Feb. 1994), 'Do you remember?', *Illyria*.

Samardžić, M. (19–20 Jan. 1991), 'Muško sam, jado jadna!' (I am Male: on the Trail of Old Customs: Sworn Virgin), *Glas*, pp. 13–14.

Smith, C. (12 Nov. 1995), 'Family under Sentence of Death', *Sunday Telegraph*.

Smith, H. (12 Feb. 1995), 'Lost Land Where Vengeance is Written in Blood', *Observer*.

Steele, J. (8 June 1998), 'We Must Rescue the Oppressed of Kosovo. And here's how to do it', *The Guardian*.

Strauss, J. (6 Feb. 1997), 'The Virgins Who Live Like Men and Treat Women as Inferior', *Daily Telegraph* p. 15.

Tansey, G. (21 July 1995), 'A Virgin Inheritance', *Times Higher Education Supplement*, p. 12.-

Thomson, I. (21 June 1992), 'Flesh and Blood in Albania', *Observer Magazine*.

Ward, L. (5 June 1995), 'Girls Will be Boys', *Telegraph & Argus*.

Woolf, L. (10 Feb. 1991), 'Let's Listen this Time', *New York Times*.

Young, A. (Dec. 1995), 'The Sworn Virgins of Albania', *Cosmopolitan* pp. 45–8.

—— (6–8 Apr. 1995), '"Sworn Virgins" Still Taking Pride in Status', *Illyria*.

—— and Prodani, A. (7 Nov. 1992), 'The Bitter Earth', *Illyria*, vol. 2, no. 143.

Index

abortion, 148
Abrahams, Fred, 148
abstinence, 6
Agolli, Dritëro, 146
agriculture, 15, 19, 34 91
Albanian Helsinki Citizens' Assembly, 150
Albanian Nongovernmental Forum, 150
Albanian Virgin, The, 64
Amazon warrior women, 55
atheist, atheism, 92, 102
avenge, avenging honour, 1, 84, 138, 140

Backer, Berit, xx, xxiv, 14, 15, 20, 21, 22, 24, 26, 33, 37n27, 38n55, 100, 113, 124
Bajraktarović, Mirko, 1, 55, 56, 61, 62
battered women's shelters, 148
berdache, *see* 'two-spirit'
Berisha, Sali, 4, 142
besa, bessa, oath, vow, 4, 6, 42, 43, 47, 51, 59, 60, 61, 64, 65, 89, 92, 140
Bjeshket e Namuna (Accursed Mountains), 100
biografi, 148, 151n8
birth control, contraception, 31, 127, 148
Black Lamb and Grey Falcon, xvii–xviii
bloodfeud, 11, 43, 49, 50–1, 64, 69, 137–46
blood revenge, 84
'in blood', 141
see also gjakmarrje and *hakmarrje*
Blumi, Isa, 131
body modification, 95
boundaries, 41, 48, 79
bridal wear, 73, 103 photo 29
bride-price, 24–5
Bringa, Tone, 101
Broken April, 44, 133, 144
burials, *see* funerals
burrneshë, 62

Byron, Lord, xxi, 131

Carver, Robert, 24, 30
Catholic, 9, 37, 61, 71, 76, 92, 93n7, 106, 121, 140 195
celibate, celibacy, 7, 61, 63, 92, 126
vow of celibacy, 43, 57, 75
chaste, chastity, 42, 69, 115
Chetta, Anton, 145
childbearing, 88
Christian, Christianity, 62, 35n8, 105, 115
clan, 13–4, 41, 43
clothing *see* dress
clothing and adornment dichotomy, 97
Communist, Communism, xxi, 6, 9, 19, 20, 31, 56, 76, 78, 86, 89, 90, 92, 99, 100, 131, 137, 139, 140, 151
fall of, 14, 88, 92, 127, 133, 143, 144, 147, 148, 150
Communist Party of Albania, 3, 54
contraception *see* birth control
Coon, Carleton, 52n72, 62
cross-dressers, cross-dressing, 5, 111–22, 124
cross-gender transformation/change, 11, 98
Çuli, Diana, 150
cult of ancestors, heaven and earth, 51
'Cult of Virgo', 55–6

d'abella, 116, 118
dashmor, 77, 108
Dayton Accords, 128n9
Dečani, xx
Demaçi, Adem, 144
Democratic League of Albanian Women, 150
Democratic Party, 4, 142
Denich, Bette, 21, 100